Our Two-fold Origin

Our Two-fold Origin

As Promise, Experience and Mission

by

Karlfried Graf von Dürckheim

Translated from the German by George Unwin

London
GEORGE ALLEN & UNWIN
Boston   Sydney

**George Allen & Unwin (Publishers) Ltd,
40 Museum Street, London WC1A 1LU, UK**

George Allen & Unwin (Publishers) Ltd,
Park Lane, Hemel Hempstead, Herts HP2 4TE, UK

George Allen & Unwin Australia Pty Ltd,
8 Napier Street, North Sydney, NSW 2060, Australia

First published in Great Britain in 1983

Translated from the German
Vom Doppelten Ursprung des Menschen
(Verlag Herder GmbH & Co. K.G. 1980)

British Library Cataloguing in Publication Data

Dürckheim, Karlfried Graf von
  Our two-fold origin.
1. Man
I. Title   II. Vom doppelten Ursprung des Menschen. English
128   BD450
ISBN 0-04-29101-7

Set in 10 on 11 point Plantin by
Computape (Pickering) Ltd, Pickering, North Yorkshire
and printed in Great Britain by
Biddles Ltd, Guildford, Surrey

Contents

Our Two-fold Origin

The Theme

Human beings are of two-fold origin, heavenly and earthly, natural and supernatural. We all know the saying. But who has learned to take it seriously, seriously as the statement of a promise, an experience and a mission?

About the 'earthly' origin of human beings nobody will have any doubt. But the assertion that they are of 'heavenly' origin is quite obviously one of those sayings that appeal only to faith. Like the content of so many other statements concerning the primordial truths of life, the truth of this too is lost on the horizon of a purely secular view of reality, in the twilight of a sphere which, belonging as it obviously does to a land of dreams, no longer has anything to do with the 'reality' we are able to grasp. But matters are otherwise.

The reality in which and out of which we actually live, and out of which we should also consciously live, reaches beyond the way of looking in which the 'natural' person's consciousness of self and the world is conceived and stirred. The saying about the dual origin of human kind expresses in all clarity and simplicity what is, and what is given, and given over to human beings to perceive as true. When they have ceased to have this truth in their inner Being and to live in accordance with it, they become sick, wicked or unhappy.

In human development, at first only the finite origin, that conditioned by the world, comes into play, and only what is connected with that is taken seriously, cultivated and held fast, in a manner that, to begin with, puts in the shade and suppresses all that comes from the infinite origin. The resolving of the tension that arises here between the earthly and the heavenly origin of mankind, and moreover its creative resolution, not an indolent dissolution, is the underlying theme of human life and the meaning of its inner course.

It is part of human nature – it is the destiny of mankind – that human beings should 'eat of the tree of knowledge' and not only develop their rational I-world-consciousness, but establish themselves in it. By this they set themselves outside the original unity of life. Because of this separation, they find themselves in a 'reality' which, in order to exist, being set now on their own feet, they themselves have to master and shape. Their original Essence, in which it is inborn in them, as promise, experience and mission, to be an individual way of the infinite Whole, is concealed from them at first; for they now support themselves as an I in the world with what they have, can do and know – and know nothing of what they are from their Essence. But remaining powerfully within it still, as their actual core, is the primordial One, which eternally ties them back and draws them home, but at the same time drives them on to rediscover It and bear witness to It in a higher Self.

Only slowly do human beings, in order to become human, detach themselves from the power of mere nature – do they develop first the primary I, which, intent only on its own security and pleasure, asserts itself; and then the 'personality', which makes the I set on values and ready to serve, and is master of its feelings and drives. But, once they have become self-reliant, everything humans do, out of themselves and out of their own strength and responsibility, continues to be blessed only when, consciously or unconsciously, they continue to be in touch with the primordial Unity of life present in their Essence. Yet this Unity becomes truly creative in a human way only when human beings discover themselves in It and, born anew out of It, detach themselves from It in order then, in the manner and language of their human existence and activity in the world as true selves, to bear witness to It in freedom.

To many ears such words may have a decidedly 'mystical' ring. But the word 'mystical', which only yesterday meant as much as non-objective, purely subjective, unreal, remote, not to be taken quite seriously, the privilege of a small group of gifted but aberrant people, is acquiring for the men and women of our time, pregnant with the future, a completely different ring. It rings, that is to say, with the central reality of our human existence.

An anthropology that has ruled us for centuries is proving too narrow. It reduces the wholeness of human beings to what they are by virtue of their five senses, their reason, their membership of a community and their commitment to wordly values and orders. Whatever goes beyond that is 'transcendent' and a matter of faith. Certainly, it is transcendent, to the extent that it oversteps the horizon of the natural world-I. But that is just what we must learn to admit to ourselves, that the human core itself oversteps the I-horizon, indeed that the transcendence inherent in human beings constitutes their *Essence*. And there is something else today: this Essence, the transcendence dwelling within us, is ceasing to be merely a matter of faith. It is entering the sphere of experience and becoming knowledge. When that happens, there is a parting of minds. And with that the dawn of a new age!

A new generation is pushing open the doors to a life that comes from the presence of the supramundane Being surging into consciousness. This is happening today in the midst of this world, corrupt in its remoteness from the Being. Even the rock-hard realism of the youth of today, apparently so lacking in respect, conceals and at the same time reveals the violence of a longing that is ready, for the sake of what is secretly and often unconsciously sought, to destroy all that is put in its way, simply because it is apparently so irrefutably there.

The world of the educationist, therapist and spiritual adviser is faced today, in respect of the generation pregnant with the future, with problems for which it has not been in any way prepared. Having grown up in a time in which it was still more or less taboo to question the authority of those set above them and when the 'intellectual goods' to be handed on were as yet undisputed, those entrusted to them for instruction and – as they thought – also for education and training did not present them basically with any real problem; for one knew, after all, what the potential certificate-holder and examination candidate, the potential official and production manager, the potential member of society and upholder of the faith had to learn. There was a prescribed notion of what it was useful to know, what abilities were necessary and what one was required to believe. Those times are gone – for the rising generation is no longer concerned primarily with what a person has, knows or can do, but with what he or she *is*. They are concerned to be allowed to be who they really are, that is, from their Essence. And what is basically moving this youth, pregnant with the future, is a sense of their infinite origin and anger at having been denied knowledge of it and access to it. And the responsible men and women of yesterday now stand before the real longing of the new era, which is replacing the modern one, with empty hands! In only a few of the 'oldsters' has their own Essence emerged with sufficient power and lack of ambiguity to break the bounds of their old anthropology, and also to keep them from having a bad conscience, which befalls so many when they depart from the forms and images of religion handed down to them and imposed upon them. But they also often stand there, to meet the penetrating look of the young, not only with empty hands, but as empty shells; not by any means because they are bad or without merit, but because they are, even as well-deserving, law-abiding, well-behaved citizens with a sense of values, existentially without ground, roots or marrow; that is, they have no sense of their heavenly origin, let alone know about it and feel, think and live out of it. So today a future full of promise rebels against a present heavy with the past. But the new prevails only gradually.

When does a priest, for instance, in hearing confession, ever hear people confess their guilt because they have gone on being 'loyal' to the order of their community even though they have heard the call, the supernatural call, which summons them beyond it and obliges them to offend against it? Certainly, it already implies a decisive step in human development when, on the strength of their consciousness, objective and receptive to values, human beings are able to evolve a mind that makes them master of their drives and feelings and their egocentric I, and fits them for service in the community and for the preservation of its order.

Offence against it is an earthly sin. But, if they become fixed in the value systems of the world, they can, if they are called from elsewhere, fall into graver sin: into sin with respect to the supramundane LIFE.

'Heavenly origin' means that we are not only children of this space-time world, but at the same time citizens in the supramundane kingdom of God. That sounds pious! But the great truths of life, to be assimilated, always need a pious cast of mind, for that alone is open to, i.e. endowed for knowing, what goes beyond the horizon of the intellect, which is indeed by its nature closed to the LIFE that cannot be comprehended rationally. That the saying about our heavenly origin and its truth might some day in a person's life become deadly serious; that the recognition of its truth as a tremendous promise and obligation might suddenly lay hold of him or her, convulse them and bid them make a completely new start – who could suspect it? That what we are in our Essence could one day dawn on us as the awakening to another Reality, in such a way that it sets us off on a new life – who among the parents, educators and leaders of our youth knows anything of that? But it is so. We must find what or who we are in our *Essence*. To that end we must die to what we are merely as children of the world, in order to be born anew to what we are from the Supramundane. This is something unheard-of, yet it is part of the *primordial knowledge* of the Great Traditions and Masters. This is the design for mankind, for all human beings in the ground of their Essence – though whether a person is called to understand it, or is even one of the chosen who are allowed to experience it and carry it out in the full sense, is another question. But the time has come to draw distinctions between minds – and to give an ever-growing number the chance of this distinction – so that those who are marked out may gain the courage to free themselves from images and formulae in which the preceding stages of the mind do indeed share in the mystery, but which obscure the full truth and hold back the development of someone who has matured sufficiently for the chance of a supernatural *experience* of Reality, of a Reality that has had its place up to now only in the faith of the natural human being.

The time has come for the hidden Being to emerge into human consciousness and tear down the walls that have obstructed It in mankind, that have prevented men and women that is, from taking It fully consciously into their experience. What people then see with the eye of their Essence differs from what they see with their natural eye as the picture revealed by X-rays differs from the picture seen by the ordinary eye, which cannot penetrate the skin. This eye, indeed, cannot even see the aura, which, as evidence of participation in the cosmic structure of vibrations, surrounds the living body of all living things.

The new vision is threefold: *experience, promise* and *mission*. People can say *yes* to it or *no*. Therein lies their freedom, the only freedom which they have! They can either seize the opportunity disclosed to them when the eye of their Essence becomes open, or waste it; they can accept the 'impossible' or hide away in the possible. They can either surrender to doubt or liberate the creative faith that will now break forth and make the impossible possible. Trust in the creative power of a faith transformed and liberated by an experience of the Being is no childlike undertaking, but not to let it in when it dawns is a betrayal of our heavenly origin. For it is in the world that mankind is required to do God's work in a human way.

The theme is stated:

We are of heavenly origin, children not only of the world but of God and called from thence to come of age. We are brothers and sisters of Christ in our Essence and partake of his Kingdom, which is not of this world.

We are called upon to become Persons, that is, to become such that the *Word* dwelling within us, as in all things, can ring out into the world. We are called to become such that we are able to demonstrate its supertemporal presence and let it be fruitful in time and space.

We are endowed and equipped not only to believe in our infinite origin, but to become aware of it in special experience and, in obedience to a call from thence, to follow the Way to a transformation by virtue of which we become able, in the midst of the world of our natural origin, to testify to the kingdom of our heavenly origin. But all this remains blocked for us so long as our indwelling light is blocked, in the darkness of a mind that acknowledges only what can be fixed objectively, and in the darkness of a medieval consciousness of sin. We must have the courage to see the light of the promise; for it is given to all and, if they have reached the necessary stage, given over to them too, to become aware that they are children of God. For this to dawn in the heart all that is required is the soberness that banishes the fear-engendering fogs of reason, and which can let in what the head can never grasp and the will never perform. To be allowed to live the great promise as a mission is the source and the meaning of the inner Way, the Way along which mankind's infinite Being becomes a binding inner Being and is able to take form in our finite existence.

I

On the Two-fold Origin of Humankind

Two kinds of suffering –
two kinds of happiness

There are two kinds of suffering and two kinds of happiness. These reveal the twofold origin of humankind. There is suffering from the threats, injustices and cruelties of this *world*, and from the inadequacy of not being able to cope with all these in the right way. And so there is happiness in experiencing security, meaning and love in this world. Rather different are the happiness and suffering of individuals through their being, or not being, at one with their supramundane *Essence*. There is suffering through separation from the Essence. And there is a happiness from being at one with the Essence in the midst of the dangers, absurdity and loneliness of the world, happiness in the experience of a secret Presence, which transforms and relieves any suffering from the world. The happiness and suffering of the *world-I*, conditioned on all sides, reveal the earthly origin of mankind. The happiness and suffering that derive from being at one, or not being at one, with the Essence reveal the supramundane origin of mankind, the God concealed within each person.

So there are also two ways of being whole. One by virtue of psycho-physical health, proper functional fitness for the world; the other by virtue of being at one with the Essence *despite* inadequacy in face of the world. The first is served by *pragmatic* therapy, whether it be physiotherapy or psychotherapy, the second by the *initiatory* art of healing. The first calls for the doctor and the physiotherapists; the second, however, for guidance along the Way, as it lives on in the tradition of the *Masters*. The continuation of this tradition, hitherto more alive in the Far East than in the West, is one of the future tasks of our time: the rediscovery of the inner Way, which begins with 'mystical' experiences – no longer merely as the privilege of individuals and the task of small secret societies and esoteric circles, but as a world-wide movement of all those who are ready for it.

The recognition of suffering in itself as real suffering, indeed, as the actual and essential suffering of humankind, signifies a turning-point in the conception, assessment and evaluation of what 'human life' really means; for only when this suffering is taken seriously does it appear what being-human means as chance, mission and promise. The concern with achievement, when it is made absolute, emerges clearly as a fatal mistake. Recognition of the meaning of inner suffering can act like a flash of lightning that lights up a person's real landscape of life, which was lying in the dark, in such a way that it invites a complete change of life: until then the person had only seen how much he or she was suffering from the world; in their suffering from not-being-at-one with their

Essence it can now suddenly dawn on them that the root of this suffering is the suppression of their divine core.

World-I and Essence

So long as people are anchored solely, to the very centre of their fabric, in their natural world-I, everything has its limit, its sense and its significance with reference to this I: the horizon of the real, objects, values, fellow human beings and the community, even God. The centring of life in the world-I governs the individual of modern times. The fact that the centre in which fundamentally everything is anchored and to which in the last analysis everything refers, that the real axis about which everything turns, is not the world-I but the supramundane Being inborn in our Essence, which transcends the horizon of the I, has become a matter of faith or else fallen completely into oblivion. With the acknowledgement of the all-transforming *experience* of the Essence, i.e. of the way in which we share in the supramundane Being, a new age is dawning for every single person who undergoes this experience, and today for a whole generation.

For the Christian this can mean that a person exists, therefore, not only as a world-conditioned I, hence only in the 'flesh', but also in the 'spirit', i.e. as an unconditioned Essence belonging to a Kingdom that is not of this world. The core-content of every experience of the Essence is an event of the soul, in which the infinite Mystery, the creative Word in us, i.e. Christ, becomes manifest as the centre of conscious life. And that is then no longer a matter of faith, but the fruit of an all-transforming experience in which a supramundane Being annuls a sorrow-filled order of existence. This turning-point marks the beginning of a New Age.

When they are as yet untransformed people believe, as soon as they have overcome their primitive nature, in themselves as independent subjects which to themselves seem 'objective' in their knowing and autonomous in their acting. They turn what is experienced into something matter-of-(f)act. What they perceive becomes for them an object, the matter of their thought, the goal of their will, given to them for their use and given over to them to fashion as they please. Everything becomes for them an object or an opponent, even the Other, even the 'Thou', even God. Everything is felt to be good or bad according to whether it can be grasped in the sense of their own conception of what is real, good or evil.

But once people break through to their Essence, jump the bounds of their I and are born anew from the Essence, the delusion that they are the lord to whom everything is subject disappears. When they become what they are at heart they feel they are related to Another, to someone Higher, who sustains, guides and calls them beyond all the distress and limitations of the world, and makes them free and powerful in face of the world in a new sense. At heart they were always so and are so beyond time, are so in their Essence, their divine origin, from which they can never fall away, and remain so even in the concealment of their world-I. It is only a question of when they will discover themselves in it; for as conscious beings they really 'are' what they are only in the way and to the extent that they become aware of their own self. With awareness of their Essence people recognise themselves as citizens of two worlds: this space-time world, limited and conditioned, and another Reality, beyond space and time, unconditioned. Each side is part of the wholeness of a human being. To recognise and admit them, each with its own concern, to suffer their conflicting character, and finally to make possible their integration and precisely in that become a complete Person – that is the mission and meaning of the *inner way*.

Between Essence and world

Natural people in their limited existence determined by space and time, create conditions for themselves which secure their continuance in the world, but at the same time endanger the outward testimony of their Essence. The skills and powers which people need to subsist happily in the world are different from those which they need for the perception of their Essence. The development of their world-powers hinders to a considerable degree the shaping and perfecting of their life from the Essence. Ties with the world are a threat to people's being-at-one with themselves. So the realisation of our existence-form takes place under circumstances the force of which generates a perpetual tension between the *life-body*, conditioned by an external destiny, and its indwelling *Essence-form*, given over to unconditional and pure outward testimony and manifestation. The *destiny-body* is a product of the world. The *Essence* is not of this world. So life is a never-ending exchange between the supramundane Essence-form inborn in us and our respective destiny-body, brought into being in the conditions of the world, in which at first all that enters from the Essence is what the world allows. The interchange of destiny-body and Essence-form is from childhood on the theme of human maturing.

From morning to night the world calls us outward. The Essence calls us constantly from within and inwards. The world requires of us knowledge and ability; the Essence that we forget again and again what we know and can do, in the service of maturing. The world requires of us that we constantly do something. The Essence requires of us that we simply give admittance to what we ourselves are in our depths. The world urges us to achieve, without ever giving any peace, and keeps us busy trying to get established, gaining a position and keeping it. The Essence requires of us that, turned towards it, we cling to nothing, so that in becoming established and settled we do not fail to find ourselves. The world keeps us talking and endlessly acting. The Essence requires that we become still and do even Doing without doing. The world forces us to think of security. The Essence encourages us to risk ourselves constantly on something new. The world yields to us if we fix it and grasp it. The Essence opens itself to us if we make no attempt to pin it down and endure what cannot be grasped. In the world we seek security. The sustaining power of the Essence proves itself if we can relinquish what secures us and holds us in the world. Only if we constantly let go afresh of what makes us rich in the world will the Essence constantly enrich us afresh. In the world we seek a secured existence and to be shielded from pain. Maturing out of the Essence goes beyond uncertainty and pain; it grows out of suffering and bears its fruit only in dying.

Human beings are faced with a double mission: to shape the world in *work* and to mature along the inner *Way*. The world requires of people that they adjust themselves to it and assert themselves with constructive vigour; that they prove themselves in it reliably and with creative power in the service of the community and of enduring values. The Being present in our Essence may require opposition to every claim of the world, and that we decide if necessary against the community. Some people may stand at the end of a development governed solely by the calling-home of the Essence; they are then not only freed from all worldly dependence, but have also released themselves from the constraint of all worldly obligation. Detached from all the world, entered into the Being, they cease while in our midst to be persons. Something of the longing for this may be found in everyone. This is the *Eastern* longing. Opposed to it is the *Western* will to live. This proves itself in the world, but can also become lost in it. The *Christian* life overrides and combines the Eastern and Western views; for it would have people perceive, grasp the truth and their heavenly origin, but bear witness to it in the midst of the world of their earthly origin. The inner Way does not then lead out of the world, is not by any means set in hostility against the 'outside'; for it has in mind the inside of everything, hence also the inside of the world and every object. The experience of becoming one with the Being in the Essence is a contradiction to being-in-the-world only so long as the inside is still not being seen also in the outside. Being anchored in the Essence is no contradiction to the demands of the world, but in fact the precondition for meeting them in the right way, i.e. in accordance with the Essence. Only from contact with the Essence *in us* can the world itself be perceived in *its* essence. 'If the eye were not sun-like, it could never glimpse the sun.' Yet the sun-eye is inborn in us; it is the heavenly eye. We must learn to open it. The heavenly eye sees through the world mirrored in the earth-eye to the heaven within it. But the earth-eye projects heaven out of the world, and makes out of the infinity dwelling within the world the firmament so distant from it.

Internal image and internal way

Human beings never want to live merely to survive. They want to live out their lives and fully realise themselves as definite someones in definite forms of themselves and their world in accordance with their Essence. And whether they know it or not, at heart they would always like to become such that they can bear witness to the supramundane Being present in their Essence, and to do so despite all the limitations of their worldly existence. When is there ever any talk of this in our education and personal guidance?

Out of the Essence inborn in them human beings experience an unremitting urge, a living obligation in their conscience and an eternal longing, to realise their core in a quite definite form, in which the Being present in their Essence can emerge unobstructed. That would only be possible, however, if there could be full harmony between what people are by virtue of their divine origin, i.e. from the Essence, and would also like to be in the world, and what they become, and in each case have to be and can only be, as conscious creatures under the limitations of the world.

What becomes apparent through all change and all becoming as an urge, as an obligation and a longing towards a definite form, as an individual and constant factor, as unquestionable Reality, is the *internal image* dwelling within us in the Essence. The internal image is our Essence understood as the binding formula for becoming that urges us unmistakably on towards a definite life-form and determines our deepest longing, but understood at the same time as the *Way* inborn in a person. So the *Essence* is fundamentally more *internal Way* than internal image. It is the Way along which alone each one of us, in a regular succession of stage and steps, can fulfil his or her life in its truth. A person's Essence *is* the way inborn in them, is their Truth and their Life, is so as promise and mission; its fulfilment is the meaning of their existence.

Transcendence

People who grow thoughtful today have become increasingly reluctant to utter the word 'God'. Not because they no longer know, or want to know, anything of God, but on the contrary at the very moment when they begin again to have some inkling of God. To them, that is to say, every word that as it were captures the Mystery, that turns it into a Something or a 'Someone', then seems too small, inappropriate, indeed absurd. And so other, more neutral words come into play, such as 'transcendence'.

When we speak of transcendence in this book what do we mean by it? We mean that which *oversteps* in an incomprehensible way the horizon of our natural knowledge and feeling; we mean the inconceivable ESSENCE of all Essences at work in all our lives, the supramundane Being beyond contradictions. We mean the LIFE, the Great Life, that is beyond life and death. We mean the all-inspiring ESSENCE, in which in our individual ways we share in our own Essences; the LIFE out of which and in which we *are*, in which and out of which alone we can really become ourselves; the LIFE, which ever and again takes us home and brings us forth afresh, and which, as our source of life, centre of meaning and true origin, seeks to appear in us and through us as the true Person and become manifest in our lives, i.e. in our knowing, fashioning and loving in the world.

We speak of this transcendent element not on the basis of a traditional faith, but on the basis of experiences in which we are touched peremptorily and beyond all doubt by a quite other dimension. These are experiences in which the Being, in Its supramundane fullness, lawfulness and unity, touches, calls, liberates and binds a person. As an I we experience this Being as a Thou. Of course in rational consciousness, in which people do their best to abstract themselves as experiencing subjects from what is experienced, they are no longer touched by anything at all. In direct experience, however, everything we experience as an I appears to us as a Thou, hence also the transcendent. If as an experiencing I we merge with what is experienced, everything loses its character as Thou. Thus in rational perception it turns into a Something – in the becoming-one of mystical experience it turns into Nothing. But afterwards, out of the power of what was experienced, comes the voice of the Great Thou.

If in direct experience we come to know transcendence as Thou, why do we not speak simply of God? Because, for those of our time who are truly perplexed and seeking, the renewal of religious life would be made difficult, indeed often even jeopardised, if the primordial experiences of the Divine, which are being granted to us afresh today, were at once pinned down in a word that recalls specific theological concepts or religious formulae, the emptying of which led to the modern crisis of faith. For this reason we speak alternatively of the other dimension, of the supramundane Life, of the divine Being, the Real beyond space and time, the Absolute, the Great Life, or write LIFE with capital letters, but always mean by it in fact only the one infinite Mystery that is inherent in us in our Essence, to become aware of which, and to be the servant and witness of which, is the human vocation.

It is the fate of human beings, in becoming aware of themselves, to fall out of their shelter in the Being. But it is their chance, through suffering from this separation, to discover anew in a higher consciousness what fundamentally they are, children of the Being. In growing up, people lose sight of their primordial home. In maturity they find it once more at a higher level. They find it again when they are touched by the mystery of their Essence in such a way that they become aware of it, and then their heavenly origin opens before them anew in a liberating and binding way, with the happiness of a homecoming. This awareness is what matters. today. But it requires a new consciousness. The necessity for this new consciousness is being felt today ever more strongly. It is precisely in an atmosphere that is becoming ever more factual and impersonal that experiences of personal significance acquire weight. They should compel due attention. Yet we know how in a flash even the most intimate personal experience can be reduced to the level of the factually recording and classifying consciousness and thus robbed of its fruitfulness! So the 'non-objective' consciousness remains undeveloped and people are denied their most important instrument for making progress along the inner Way. The finding of this instrument, a consciousness in accordance with the Essence, is the task that stands at the beginning of the inner Way.

Two kinds of knowledge

There is knowledge conditioned by time and knowledge beyond time. The knowledge that serves mastery of the world is constantly undergoing further development. One finding supersedes another. What was discovered yesterday is no longer adequate today. But the knowledge of a Lao-tse is a wisdom that is as valid today as it was in his own time. So there is a world-knowledge that develops with progress and a primordial knowledge about the Essence and its Way that is timeless.

Mankind's eternal stock of wisdom refers to the Essence in human beings, to their inner becoming and to their relation with the supramundane Life. Here is something living and traditional which is independent of space and time. It is something which undoubtedly always manifests as well as veils itself in the garb of appearances, contradictions and stages of development conditioned by space and time – but which gleams nevertheless through all outer covering as the One, as the LIFE beyond space and time. This supertemporal Essence of all things, the eternal but hidden source of authenticity, which for one who has the Essence-eye shines nevertheless through all appearances, is contained in a primordial knowledge and primordial conscience, which is inborn in human beings and unconsciously their own, and to which they can awaken in special experiences. To the microscope of reason, even the keenest, this is closed, for the microscope always looks in the wrong direction.

There is also the primordial knowledge, which is, renewed in experience, of the conditions in which the Being veils Itself in humans, and also of the other conditions in which conversely it can emerge in them, become conscious and through them take form in the world. This knowledge comes to us in the enlightened knowledge of the sages and Masters, in the core-content of the creation-myths of all peoples and in the guiding wisdom of the founders of all the great religions and their authentic witnesses. In our own time it is cropping up out of the distress of people who had forgotten their heavenly origin, who are almost going under as a result and who are rediscovering it in the experience of their Essence, i.e. in 'transcendence as experience'.

The knowledge that always has only temporary validity and lies in progress refers to the world. It is founded on natural experience, is apprehended by the objective consciousness and flows into natural science and technology, through which human beings perceive the world objectively and master it according to their will. The primordial knowledge that outlives the ages but must always be discovered anew refers to the human Essence, to human distress and promise. It is founded on supernatural experiences and flows into the wisdom in which humans perceive themselves in the Being and change their vocation accordingly.

Wave, leaf and tendril

To recognise that one is a part of the Whole, indeed that one is oneself the Whole in the way of a part, requires a special consciousness. One requires a consciousness that is different from the one in which the Whole in which one is, and which is in a person, is there as a confronting Something from which one distinguishes one's own self as a separate entity.

Three examples:

If one said to a wave, 'You are after all in the sea,' the wave might reply, 'That's what you say.' 'Where then,' one might ask the wave, 'does the sea begin for you?' 'Right here,' says the wave, 'here, where my foams ends. I am here, and the sea is there!' If one then went on to ask, 'And you yourself, are you not yourself a wave of the sea, are you not yourself the sea in the way in which it appears as a wave?' the wave might well *understand* this with its head, but in order to feel what the living truth of the words mean a consciousness is required in which the sea is no longer merely 'there', no longer present merely objectively and opposingly as a confronting something, but taken up into the view of an intrinsic consciousness. Only in this will the wave become *inwardly* and non-objectively aware of its own being-the-sea. Only in this consciousness can it become conscious of what is closed to it in the objective consciousness.

So it is too with the leaf and the tree. If the only idea the leaf has of its being-a-leaf is to see itself as separate from the tree, then of course it must be afraid when autumn comes, dries it up and eventually blows it from the tree, and lets it fall to earth and finally vanish into dust. But if the leaf were to realise that it is itself the tree in the way of a leaf, and that the yearly life and death of the leaf is part of the tree, then the leaf might well have a different consciousness of life. But to recognise this truly from within requires again that intrinsic consciousness in which it can become aware of itself in its Essence, and merge with it, as a way of the Whole that lives within it. Only when it feels itself also as tree in the way of a leaf will it carry out, without resistance or dismay, along with all the other leaves, the coming-into-being and going-out-of-being in which the tree itself lives out its life in an eternal 'dying and becoming'.

So is it too with the tendril on the vine. 'Yes,' says the tendril, 'I hang on the vine. I am a tendril and there, when my stalk ends, the vine begins.' So it says when it sees reality, like an as yet unawakened human being, only in the scheme of 'I-am-I' and 'that-is-that'. But it might also dawn on the tendril one day, quite from within, that the vine is in fact also in it and it in the vine, in fact that it shares in the vine – in fact that it is itself the vine in the special way of this tendril and that its actual Essence, its source of life, the root of its form and its home is the vine, hence the Whole of which it is a part. And that only when it really had this in its inner being would it have reached a self-awareness in accordance with its Essence. But that is the very thing that requires the other consciousness.

Human origin is of two kinds – heavenly and earthly. But only when human beings become aware of themselves *inwardly*, like the wave of its being-the-sea, the leaf of its being-the-tree and the tendril of its being-the-vine, as the Whole dwelling transcendently and mysteriously within them, as life, meaning and home, will they *know* about their heavenly origin, as experience, promise and mission, and need no longer merely believe in it.

II

The Man and Woman of Our Time

The compulsion to achieve – and its shadow

'Help me, Professor, I'm in a bad way! I don't know what's the matter. I'm as fit as a fiddle, play plenty of games, I've got all the money I want, and everything's fine at work and at home. Yet I'm tormented by fear – what of, I don't know; I have feelings of guilt – why, I don't know; and I suffer from loneliness, though I'm not alone. What's the matter with me?'

'Have you any kind of golden rule for life,' I ask him, 'something which decides how you look at things?'

'Oh yes,' he replies, 'I've got that. Just three words. They're hanging up all round me at work: "Achievement is all!"'

'So,' I ask in return, 'achievement is all?'

He repeats it with a mixture of pride and defiance, but now with a touch of uncertainty.

'Have you never heard anything of an inner Way,' I go on, 'to which a man is committed no less than to his visible work? Have you never heard anything about the need for spiritual progress and its blessings, an inner maturing, without which there is no inner peace?'

At these words my patient's face clouds over, and he makes a gesture that is both defensive and dismissive. 'You mean religion,' he says, 'or something spiritual? My dear chap, people like me have no time for that; one can't make machines with that, or get on in the world!'

The answer is typical and reveals the whole abysmal nature of the situation. These people, often industrious, well educated, respectable and well-meaning people, are so caught up in the achievement madness, i.e. the madness of being able to go through life and answer for it only in the name of successful achievement, that they seriously believe they must suppress the whole of their spirituality. The outcome then is an achievement-animal, harnessed solely to the demands of the world, which in its one-sided development is a caricature of what a human being really is and should increasingly become: a unity of body, mind and soul. If one could paint such people, one would have to depict them with gigantic heads, puffed-out chests, limbs of steel functioning quite mechanically, not combining organically but held together and guided artificially by a hard will. In the middle, where the directing, organising and inspiring centre should be, there would be very little, in fact only a hollow space in which, encased in a fearful and easily injured I, the actual Essence leads a shadow-life! In spite of all they have, know or can do, people who correspond to this picture remain children. Outwardly adults, but inwardly immature, lacking self-control and full of illusions.

They are helpless before the forces of destiny and finally go under in life because they have failed to find themselves. Then, from their neglected Essence gasping for breath come those feelings of incomprehensible fear, guilt and emptiness which are being experienced today by so many of those who appear from the outside to be at the peak of their development. Others, who cannot see within, may admire the façade. Behind it live unhappy people whose spiritual suffering and lack of inner stillness, no less than their baneful influence, are the price they pay for having remained immature, through failing to become aware of themselves in their Essence. They know nothing of their heavenly origin, or of the mission and meaning that have been given to them with it. All talk of it is to them sound and fury. Reality belongs only to what is valid in the world. The means to that is achievement!

But is there no need for achievement?

In praise of achievement

Only in achievement do people learn to meet the demands of life, the demands of the 'world', both of nature and of the community.

Only by achieving something are people able to stand up to life and lead a life of meaning. Only on the strength of their achievements can they master life, can they harness the forces of nature. Only by their achievements do people mould and prove themselves as useful and unselfish members of the community! Every achievement that is valid in the world, in which people serve a business or a community, forces them also to set aside their selfish I and orient their activity towards objective demands and standards. Only in this way do people become personalities, i.e. reliable supporters and custodians of the values entrusted to them by the world.

In all criticism of pure achievement, therefore, the principle of achievement as such can never be called in question, nor can its significance for a person's education, training and development be diminished. But for the achievement principle to remain beneficial and healthy one thing is necessary: it must not become the sole principle of life, or fixed as absolute, but must remain embedded in the whole of human life. If it occupies the centre of the whole, its effect in the world is disastrous, and mankind becomes sick. The blame for that, however, does not lie with the achievement principle but with human beings, who, in their one-sided pursuit of achievement, forget their inner Essence and maturity. It is not the achievement principle that perverts mankind but mankind that perverts the achievement principle.

Achievement in the world can serve the Supramundane in three ways:

1 by creating something that, as deed, product or organisation, gives out something supramundane;
2 by creating or recognising in the world the conditions in which people can unfold and live in accordance with their Essence;
3 by being carried out not only for the sake of what comes out of it into the world, but of what 'comes in' from it for the achiever.

The external measure of every achievement is its result, hence what 'comes out' of it. Its inner measure should be what people gain from it, in the preparation and carrying out of achievements, for themselves, i.e. for their inner growth.

The lack of stillness

The man and woman of our time lack stillness, outer stillness and, even more, inner stillness, i.e. the frame of mind tha-noise'; indeed, even more: for which outer noise can be a background that highlights inwardly what cannot be disturbed by any sound. This is true stillness. It is a disposition of the mind – a state of the soul – in which the noise of the world is transformed into a 'backdrop of sound' before which inner stillness first develops fully and becomes conscious.

There is the stillness of life and the stillness of death. The stillness of death is where nothing moves any more. The stillness of life is where nothing holds back the movement of change any more. This stillness is one of the fruits of the inner Way.

People who emanate stillness, because it is still within them, have become rare. In place of stillness, which comes from being anchored in the Essence, a simulated 'calmness', an outer 'shutting-oneself-down' has appeared. The outer calmness that comes from self-discipline, however, is something different from the stillness proclaimed by an inner state of mind, which needs no act of will in order to be there. It is also something different from the 'beer-calmness' of a phlegmatic person, under which no life pulsates any more. There are people, certainly, with a 'thick skin', and there are others who have in their nature an all-harmonising vibration-formula that charms away all friction. Through their lack of sensitivity and responsiveness they are spared disturbing emotion. In them, the disturbing impression that excites others goes up in smoke, as does the inner impulse, before it can ever gain any depth. But the stillness of such people is insipid and shallow. Force, depth and radiance are found only in the stillness that reveals the presence of the Essence, which has its home in the Being beyond contradictions. True stillness is a force from our heavenly origin. Where it emanates from a person, it has an effect that is both relaxing and ordering. Without any words, it brings those around that person more to themselves. Under the influence of the Essence expressed in it, waves of excitement subside. Unpleasantness melts away, and questions are answered as if of their own accord. In true stillness the voice of the LIFE becomes audible.

Living in the human being is a secret knowledge that true stillness, for which the soul longs, is more than just an agreeable lack of noise, more than a mere restful counterpart to the restlessness and overtaxing of the body, more than a mere prerequisite for all life of the mind or the condition for spiritual health. It is a knowledge that genuine stillness is fundamentally more than the prerequisite or condition for a happy life; that it is, rather, synonymous with the experience of life itself being fulfilled! Even in our own time, this primordial human experience is not yet completely buried: when people are truly happy they are always still, and conversely, when they are able to become truly still, only then does true happiness unfold in them.

People differ in their receptivity to stillness and in their readiness to make sacrifices for it. They differ for reasons of age, maturity and character. A person who has been tried by life is closer to it than someone who has not yet been through the school of suffering. A person turned to the outside is further from it than someone who has been given the Way to the inside. A peasant knows more about stillness than someone who revels in town life; but someone to whom life has denied natural stillness is often far closer to the longing for stillness, and so to its deeper experience, than someone who – still at one with nature – enjoys it entirely as a matter of course.

All over the world peasants try out strangers entering their house for the first time with the 'test of stillness'. It is not by any words of introduction that peasants measure a stranger's human worth. Noisy behaviour and any attempt to look them straight in the eye are to them suspect. Turned to one side, they listen in to the silence emanating from the atmosphere surrounding the stranger. It is the eloquent aura of a person's enveloping substance that they consult, the silent vibrations that emanate from a person, beyond anything the person may do or say.

It is the art of all Masters to try people out not by what they can do or say but by the degree and quality of the stillness that emanates from them, for their equilibrium and inner order, their rank and inner stage.

'Maturity? What is it?' Satomi Takahashi, the philosopher of Sendai, began to answer me once, fell silent, and then said quietly with a smile: 'A vast stillness.'

And Søren Kierkegaard, the great seeker, put it like this: 'As his prayer became ever more devout, he had ever less and less to say. Finally, he became quite still. He became still; indeed, what is if possible an even greater contrast to speaking, he became a listener. He thought at first that to pray was to speak; but he learned that to pray was not only to keep silent, but to listen. And so it is: to pray does not mean to listen to oneself speaking. To pray means to become still, and to be still, and to wait until the Praying God is listening.'

Today's distress

The distress in which men and women find themselves today, as 'heirs to the modern age', is due above all to the fact that the axis of life about which everything turns is no longer the divine Being, present in the human Essence and inner being, but men and women themselves, trapped in their world-I. The meaningful centre is no longer the Whole that embraces and is at work through all human life, is no longer God, but men and women, who by virtue of their rational powers think they can stand on their own and by virtue of their capacity for selfless service think they are of value on their own. But this implies a secularisation of the whole of life, a profanation of the sense of existence through the loss of any anchorage in the transcendent.

To the degree that life is reduced for human beings to a rationally knowable and organisable structure, whose smooth functioning is the source of all well-being, to that degree do people become, even when they serve 'higher values' or society, mere functionaries. They reduce themselves to carriers of rationally comprehensible, measurable and quantitatively evaluable functions and achievements. This depersonalisation of life means more, and something other, than the containment of the purely individual element and the private I necessary in every community; more too than the demand for selfless achievement that is made by every organised society. The 'deep-person', who cannot be comprehended rationally, is no longer taken seriously, and is thereby excluded as a determining factor. It becomes a nothing; for reality in our human world belongs only to what we take seriously.

The exclusion of the personal means not only a disregarding of the secret of individuality but also a denial of the transcendent depths, of the

Essence. The existential wholeness of human beings is thus robbed of its core and centre; for in their core human beings are something that points beyond them. And human beings are in their true centre only when they remain, even in the life-form of their being-in-the-world, in accordance with the supramundane Whole in which fundamentally they are meant to be at home in their individual ways.

A particular feature of the lapse of human wholeness lies in the overemphasis of the masculine, active, fixing, setting, differentiating, ordering and defining functions of the human spirit; as against which the relaxing, receptive, connecting, unconfining, secretly supportive, sheltering and transforming feminine forces come off badly. With this goes a monstrous narrowing of vision: through the prism and focus of masculine consciousness, which fixes things objectively only and is concerned with possession, security and achievement, the Logos is reduced to Ratio, the cosmic forces to psycho-physically 'comprehensible' drives, and love to a way of clinging – and everything, everything becomes an 'object', a manipulable thing, even human beings.

What is decisive, however, is the denial thereby given to the transcendent depths of our personal being and the prevention of its testimony in the world. The objectively incomprehensible Essence, the way in which the supramundane Being is present in us, out of which fundamentally we alone truly exist, to the manifestation of which we are destined each in his or her particular way, and on the perception of which all maturing also depends – this Essence in each of us has been sacrificed today to the world-I. Where consciousness of reality is governed by Ratio everything that does not fit into its scheme, or which oversteps it, hence to all 'transcendence', is inconvenient or illusory and is banished to the realm of the unreal, assigned to the domains of pure faith, imagination or metaphysical speculation.

But whatever men and women think to know with any validity, or do with any permanence, with their natural gifts only and without contact with their Essence, rigidifies or falls apart again; for it lacks the breath of the supernatural, creative-redemptive Life that fructifies all the reality of the world.

The maturing of men and women, the blessing of their works and their true freedom and coming of age depend on their giving admittance to their Essence, i.e. to the individual manifestation of the supramundane Life present in their worldly bodies; on their accepting it into their responsible consciousness; and on their not letting go of the golden thread to it even in their wordly activity. So the very situation in which men and women believe they can arbitrarily disregard their Essence, in which they set up as their final authority a consciousness of reality that has no place for transcendence, represents the summit of human immaturity, bondage and minority. Inevitably, they fall ever more into suffering, in which the suppression of their Essence makes itself known.

I-growth and Essence

The problem of becoming an I is a fundamental theme of human existence. Acquiring the right I determines a person's right relationship to the world, to his or her self and to transcendence. But just as all psychology in the last analysis leads to valid results only from a metapsychological standpoint, so too is there a prospect of seeing correctly the problem of acquiring the right world-I, or of failing to do so, only if one approaches the whole problem in the light of the Supramundane, i.e. of mankind's transcendent home and destiny.

In the beginning and in the end, in the origin and in the unfolding of all life stands the transcendent 'I AM'.

Behind, in and above everything that exists human beings sense the great 'I AM' of all life as the 'stillness of the divine Being', out of which all life comes forth, into which it returns, creation–redemption–creation without end. Understood thus, the great 'I AM' means the All-embracing and All-pervading, whose 'Word' dwells in all that exists and gives it corporeal form, but gives to human beings at the same time corporeal consciousness, and by virtue of this consciousness and this form seeks to become manifest in a human way in the world.

Every single creature is destined to live out in its own way in the foreground the 'I AM' of the divine Ground; so too are human beings, in the way that is determined by their particular character. The thematic material of human life is marked by the forms and stages of its growth in consciousness. In these the great 'I AM' manifests itself in the many and various ways of saying 'I am', reveals itself, by first veiling itself in order to emerge one day, in a person's suffering at this veiling, as all-transforming Light. 'I am', experienced portentously as all-redeeming and all-transforming depth, is also the end to which the great meditation leads, lived as an exercise in transformation.

Someone who has arrived at his or her natural self-awareness does not say 'I am', but 'I am I'! The I of this 'I am I' is the centre of natural human consciousness, an obvious prerequisite and component in the wholeness of fully developed human life. It is the basis of world-conditioned and world-related self-awareness and the centre point of the objective world-view of the natural person. So long as this I is not there, a person is still bound up in the cosmic orders, sheltered by them, but also exposed to the forces of life and not as yet a subject. Thus in early childhood, and where primitive people are still immersed in the integral life of their community and nature, there can be no question of proper I-consciousness any more than of a consciousness of the 'world'. Immersed in their environment, they live solely out of their participation in the sheltering and demanding whole.

The 'I am I' marks awareness of a firmly held identity, by which three different things are assumed:

1   I am I and want to remain so – hence the *standing fast* of the I through all change;
2   I am I, something particular, destined to a particular form – hence the specialness of being I, *different* from others;
3   I am I and preserve myself in face of the other (thou), i.e. the self-preserving *apartness* and opposition of being I in face of the other.

As people become aware of this I, i.e. insofar as they are now determined by this awareness, they emerge from the original and non-contradictory unity of life. From the standpoint of their 'I am I' such people, who even now still feel at one with their body, experience life in opposites, thus in the opposition of I and world, of here and there, of before and after, of above and below, of heaven and earth, spirit and nature, and so on. So long as people identify themselves completely with this I, they will perceive everything, and take it seriously, only in the categories of this I. Anything that cannot be apprehended in the system of space and time, identity and causality, cannot be perceived and taken seriously as *reality*. If this I were to be taken away and to disappear, what in fact would still be there? Nothing would be 'there' any more, says the 'Western' man or woman, who identifies with this I. Then and only then, says the wisdom of the East from time immemorial, does the Reality dawn that is 'not of this world'. But from the standpoint of the I, of course, only the former is declared to be the one real reality. The Reality that oversteps, i.e. transcends, all the limits of that reality is beyond the five Ws, the What, When, Where, Whence and Whither! How do we know about it? From experiences in which the *vehicle* of consciousness is not the fixing I but a form of consciousness that intrinsically feels, preserves and fructifies! It is the consciousness in which the Essence enters the inner being. But the more people establish themselves in their world-I and their positions, the deeper grows the opposition between their I, consolidating itself in its will to endure and in its system of consciousness, and their Essence, pressing unremittingly towards change.

In their Essence human beings share, each in his or her individual way, in the Being; so too in their little life, limited by birth and death, do they share in the great LIFE beyond space and time. The 'Essence' is the way in which the infinite human origin is present in the finite human state, conditioned by a person's I. The Essence is the way in which the Being in a person presses to become manifest in the world in a certain form. Thus the Essence is also the formative principle, the internal way inborn in human beings to the form intended for them. This world-form will also always be an I-form. But the Essence can only become manifest in its corporeal world-I to the degree that the person, in all his or her conditioning through the world, has yet remained, or become again, transparent in 'body and soul' for their Essence. There is thus a successful I and an unsuccessful I. A person's I is successful only to the degree that it does not prevent, but on the contrary makes possible, and to a certain extent guarantees, transparence for the Essence to become manifest in a living form appropriate to it. But a person's usual development as a conscious being implies that the world-I forming under the conditions of the world, the I which, through the predominance of the consciousness that establishes everything, creates static systems and in order to survive builds up its positions, stands in the way of the outward testimony of the form that is in accordance with the Essence only in never-ending change. Participation in the living fullness, lawfulness and unity of the LIFE that enjoins eternal change is woefully obstructed by such a consciousness – and yet it is only thanks to, and with, such a consciousness that a person is able to live and develop and have any creative force in the world.

The system of consciousness centred in the I means at first a view of life in which the Greater Life is concealed. It is the system of consciousness of the natural origin, which to begin with puts the heavenly origin in the shade. This brings specifically human suffering. Yet in its very limitedness, which brings the suffering, this consciousness becomes the cause of an awakening in a person sooner or later of a longing for the original unity of life. And then one day it also forms the background against which, in certain experiences, the emergent Being, which shatters the limits of the I-world, can stand out and become known as the 'Wholly Other'. Without the evolution of an I-world made up of contradictions there is no fruitful 'experience' of the transcendence beyond contradictions. To receive it again in their inner being after their defection, to discover it again as the source of life, as the root of all that gives meaning, and as the sheltering home that is indeed not of this world, and then to allow it to become manifest in the midst of experience, is the destiny of human beings, is the secret nerve of all human striving, all their search for happiness, fulfilment and peace; whatever contradicts it is – the source of their distress. The mere fact of this craving, this longing and search represents in itself an *experience* of a determining, causative Force full of promise at work through everything, which takes the experience, as an incontrovertible datum, out of the realm of mere *belief* in transcendence into that of imperative *knowledge* – though only for *those* people who are able, without fear of retribution, to break the shackles and limits of the purely objectively determined consciousness and the image-world that has arisen and hardened with its help.

The longing for deliverance from suffering from the limitations of a consciousness anchored only in the world-I drives people to reflect one day on the nature of the consciousness-structure of the I-reality that hems them in. This reflection is the precondition for their divining not only the Way that leads beyond the I-shell, through taking seriously experiences in which the Being speaks, to integration with the Being, but also the Way that leads to the formation of an I that will be in the service of the Being and not in opposition to It. For this right I is what matters in the end! It is not a question of destroying every I, but of liberation from the false I and the development of a world-I permeable to the Essence.

The contradiction between the I clinging in and to the world and the Essence bound to the Being forms an inherent and inalienable state of conflict in human beings that has to be lived in a dialectical process, in which humans have always to become conscious afresh of their roots in the Being and their ties that go back to It, in order to prove themselves in the world again and again as an I that bears the Being. People's worldly effectiveness in accordance with the Being depends not only on their ever-renewed reflection on their ties with the Being, but just as much on the decisiveness with which they resist the temptation to become absorbed either wholly in the world or wholly in the Being, and are ready on their own responsibility and in their own form to bear witness to the Being independently in the world. Humans are called upon to continue God's work in a human way in their human world, i.e. to let the supramundane Being take form in the world in a human way. That is the meaning of their independence and freedom and the fruit of their suffering from their 'defection', when they recognise it and turn back.

The strength of the primary world-I, its basic concern and its 'principle', is *fixing*. People become Is by thinking 'I am I', thus establishing their identity with themselves. Only through this do they acquire their 'position', their 'standing'. To this I-standing the 'world' takes shape as 'op-position' and then from every standing as a fixed 'ob-ject'. 'World' signifies a structure of established elements in itself, standing on its own, and, from one's own standpoint, standing against oneself. Previously, life was lived only in complex involvement with what was experienced as 'environment', and not yet as a detached world standing on its own. To find their own firm standing in the I and an objective, firm-standing world is necessary to human beings. It becomes fatal to them, however, when they try to settle down in it alone and 'dig themselves in' for ever. The pursuit of a theoretically or practically firm-standing reality that exists independently of the human subject is a characteristic theme of human life. Against that another theme is at work all the time, in which the human subject seeks deliverance from his or her suffering from the world.

Wondering and suffering

There are two motive roots from which the human spirit grows and flourishes, perfects itself and is endangered. One is *wondering*, the other is *suffering*. Both motive forces are undoubtedly at work in every human being. But one must learn to distinguish the particular effect and strength of each, and to recognise the danger of one-sidedness in either, so that one can then see them together in the right way and coordinate them productively.

Wondering poses the questions: 'What is that? How does it all hang together? Where does it come from? What will follow from it?' With such questions people put themselves each time in face of something other, put what stands in face of them in the foreground of their interest, whether for knowing, mastering, shaping or perfecting. In face of it the questioners themselves must then step into the background. People struck by wonder step back in face of what is worthy of wonder, as soon as it becomes worth knowing. Where on the other hand suffering becomes the agent of the mental movement, the authentic, decisive and guiding factors of life become the individuals struck by suffering themselves! The other, standing in face of them, has its significance, not in what it is in itself, but in how it helps or endangers, attracts or hurts, calls in question or confirms. And in this significance it becomes increasingly the occasion for the individuals to search into the depths, independent of the world, of their own interior, i.e. for going inward.

People touched by wondering are concerned with a reality that exists independently of themselves. People stirred by suffering see in all reality what affects themselves, for the centre of the reality that moves them is they themselves.

In wondering as in suffering the fathomless LIFE in human beings comes pressing into consciousness of its own accord. Out of wondering it takes form in the objectively perceiving consciousness of the 'head', seeking clarity; in suffering, as the understanding, intrinsic consciousness of the 'heart', seeking deliverance. From the one grows the mission for perceiving and shaping a reality pictured by human beings as independent, functioning of its own accord or as valid work to be done, hence for an objective reality relieved of all the dross of feeling subjectivity. From the other grows the mission for the maturing of a subject who is freed from all delusion of imagining an objective world, and whose never-resting inner being thus accepts imperturbably the unshaped, dangerous world that is in constant change. In the latter the picture of life is governed by the idea of a subject finally freed from all world-reality; in the former, on the other hand, by the idea of a view, purged of all subjective experience, of a reality subsisting in itself, i.e. ontologically comprehensible, which is to be demonstrated, served and believed in. The mind is thereby directed towards something that endures, that withstands the passage of time, whether because it is made of 'marble', i.e. of imperishable material, or whether because it is true as a 'form' or because it embodies in its content as work of art or knowledge a supertemporal meaning and gives reality to a supertemporal value. The world itself, if it corresponded to its highest idea, would then be a well ordered, enduring structure, functioning smoothly for its human beeings, of technically mastered facts and smoothly functioning organisations and human relations which formed a perfect whole.   Predominant here is the final form of a world which in its unshadowed harmony shines ultimately in the light of an eternity exempt from all transience. To be committed to it is thus the motive source and legitimation of all development towards the perfect human being. For being humanly complete is then fulfilled in the service of such a final form.

In the model of life that derives from suffering, on the other hand, the opposite of objective reality, namely particular subjects in their greatest depth, is the region of final reality. Not a something independent of all consciousness, but a consciousness purged of every something, i.e. freed from the power of objects, is here the promising motive force of human life. Not something that as the objectively real is in the end detached from human beings and inaccessible to human experience, but conversely a most inward Something, which as the Essence of all essences reveals itself only indeed to the subject's deepest experience in a higher consciousness, and is given over to this experience, and which, when It becomes experience, fulfils the meaning of human existence by representing the greatest freedom, deliverance and the deepest peace. When the deepest experience is itself the scene and refuge of the highest Reality, the idea that an objective world, i.e. one that is removed from experience, is the final reality is a delusion. When what is being sought is a consciousness no longer clouded by anything in the nature of an object, the fixing of a something, hence even the development of the natural, objective consciousness, is the beginning of all aberration. When this consciousness becomes absolute, it constitutes the fundamental error of mankind.

Human life is always occupied with both, with intellectual activity aiming at what can be established, and with suffering longing for deliverance. When one of the two motives no longer admits the other, human life is in danger of going under or of becoming meaningless. Losing the way and the suffering that results thereby are then indeed the precondition for a conscious finding of the right truth and the right way, along which in the end the integration of the growing powers of the mind, from suffering and from wondering, takes place. The predominance of the longing for deliverance characterises the attitude to life in the Far East. The prevalence of an intentness on 'objective reality' determines the face of Western civilisation. Christian thought is based on a conception of life that resolves the contradiction, redemptively and at the same time creatively. Here then the knowing and shaping of the objective world stands in the service of the Being, pressing towards the light in the suffering human as subject, and this in its turn becomes the factor that gives meaning and creative force to all change in the world. This 'integral' life, given over to the human being as Person, is in the last analysis the yardstick by which all stages of becoming are to be judged and measured.

Wondering, suffering – the motive roots of the human spirit! Wondering appears first, as the force that fulfils itself in human beings increasingly in the rational knowing and mastering of the objectively comprehensible world. Suffering appears by way of opposition, first as the distress that in the end gives people the right to despise the world for the sake of their own deliverance. And yet this is not so. As soon as people see not only their entirely personal suffering but also that of the rest of suffering humanity, they are forced to perceive and take seriously the world that is to be rationally known and mastered. The questions that spring from wondering do lead without doubt to the development of the Ratio and the 'objective reality', remote from feeling, that is associated with it; but as a primordial phenomenon wondering is at the beginning and in the end the expression of the 'Super-reality' that eludes all Ratio, which presses towards the light in our 'head-reality' no less than in our sorrowful 'heart-reality'. The impulses of life that arise from both wondering and suffering clearly have one thing in common: to serve the liberation and deliverance that human beings always and everywhere implore from their gods. Perhaps, however, they should realise for once that the meaning of their life, driven on in wondering as in suffering, should be rather to free the divine element imprisoned within them from the captivity imposed on it by their earthly origin.

The successful world-I

The only form of I that could be called a successful world-I would be one in which a person found his or her happiness and freedom as a witness and servant of the Being. This would be a living form that remained transparent for the Essence, that swung freely under all conditions about the axis of its self-becoming in accordance with the Essence, and remained open to change in all its independence, permeable in all its form, and in form in all its permeability. This 'permeable form' and 'formed permeability' is in the end the purpose of all spiritual exercise.

The successful world-I has passed, therefore, beyond the first function of I-becoming – the acquisition of an independence and assertiveness based on the natural drives and the capacity for rational knowledge – to the stage of a personality open to 'values'. Over and above that, people with a successful world-I have found touch with the Essence. Out of what they *are* in the Essence, and not just from what they have, can do and know, they are confident that they can cope with suffering, and they have faith in an overriding meaning, i.e. in a fullness and order of Life underlying all things. By virtue of the unity of the Being sheltering them in the Essence, they also feel, through all contradictions, at one with the world. Of course even in a successful I, people live in the world by an orientation to what is for them established. But they come to terms with the never-ending changeability and dangerousness of life, and even its transience, to the extent that they are not completely identified with the I's will to endure, but from the Essence remain open to the eternal change inherent in life, of which going out of the world is as much a part as coming into it. 'The wages of sin is death' does not then mean 'Because you have sinned you must die', but death as *terror* is the answer to people who have cut themselves off in such a way that their will to endure leads them to resist going out of the world, which is as much a part of life as coming into it.

For people with a successful I, life is ordered not in circles round a position in the world, but in striving for transparence for the supra-mundane Essence and the change demanded by it. The succesful I is not a contradiction of the Essence, but the instrument of its manifestation in the world. For 'successful I' means the form of human existence in which people are able to testify to the Essence in the world.

People who have a successful I do not live, therefore, just by virtue of their I. They do indeed *live* as an I related to the space-time world, but they *exist* out of an Essence-Ground that points beyond the I and its being-in-the-world. The centre of their worldly system of consciousness, bearing witness to their earthly origin, is indeed the objectively fixing I, yet this is overridden by the Wholeness, centred in their heavenly origin, of a growing Self which, with direct experience of the manifesting urge of the Essence, puts the I in the service of the Being.

Through its dependence on the I-principle human development is open to a twofold danger. The world-I, where it is too dominant, may prevent admittance of the centre out of which speaks the Wholeness of LIFE; its static systems may block the approaches to the Essence and the breath of the Greater Life. Or, where not enough I is developed, there may be a lack of that form, that shape, without which the Essence cannot become 'human' and fit for the world.

If people remain bound to their Essence, their life 'plays' out of a mysterious elasticity in their depths round the firm and yet flexible axis of never-ending change. In the unsuccessful I this is not to be found, for it is either constantly anxious about 'positions', in rigid shells, or it wavers without form or direction, hither and thither, and is then never far from disintegration. It lacks containment from the Essence, which precludes imprisonment in rigid shells just as it does the threat of disintegration.

There are two different ways in which human beings experience the transcending of their world-I to something more comprehensive: as the irruption of the Being as Logos and as a widening through the influx of cosmic forces. Both lie in store in the process of becoming a Person in the real sense.

Sharing in the forces of the cosmos or Logos that override the world-I is in itself impersonal and non-personal. The earth-forces are pre-personal, the spirit-forces suprapersonal. Overstepping their natural I, people can settle in either and function out of either, without already being Persons themselves in the highest sense, or without giving themselves as Persons. They can be gripped by the forces of the earth as by the forces of the spirit; their little I can be taken up, indeed sucked up, by either in turn, so that they are there and functioning as though I-less, not just in an ecstasy or state of inspiration, but even in their responsible, everyday activity (e.g. as healers or spiritual advisers). And yet in such activity, which may be very beneficial, they still do not give themselves completely. They themselves as unique individuals, real only in their particular bodies conditioned in a thousand ways, inseparable from their personal destinies, individuals compounded of their happiness and their distress, their hopes and their fears; in a word, they themselves as human beings are still not really there at all in such healing work. All true teachers, all doctors, all therapists, and in particular all spiritual advisers know the peculiar jump that takes place in their relation to the person committed to them at that moment when they cannot do other than open themselves to the one facing them, and then, through their official dress, emerge as whole people and so encounter the other as themselves. Despite all the dangers connected with this, they know and feel it: only then do they reach the other truly from Person to Person.

Of course, for anything like this to be of healing value, the giving and guiding individuals must themselves have attained to a centre as Persons. It is not very easy for this first really personal engagement to take place precisely when such people, whether in league with the cosmic or spiritual forces, have become as it were I-less. They then live, love, work and function either out of their earthly centre or their heavenly centre, but not yet out of the centre of their 'being-in-the world' as Persons. They function, perhaps helpfully, but pre-personally, like many non-medical healers or even impersonally like many priests. 'A human being, seen as a whole, i.e. a complete human being, is not just an intermediate link between heaven and earth, between nature and spirit, and now this now that, but the union of both in an enlightened consciousness.'*

Defective forms of I

There are two faulty developments of the I. In one people lose themselves in an I-shell that has become immobile. In the other people lose themselves because they have not arrived at any compact I-form at all.

THE RIGID I-SHELL

The defective form of 'rigid I' results from a 'taking-the-bit-between-its-teeth' of the fixing I-principle. It is part of the nature of the I to establish things, to hold fast to what is established and to assert itself in something settled – in the practical sphere of daily life, in the realm of theoretical knowledge, or in the forms of ethical behaviour.

People who have become trapped and hardened in the shell of their world-I hold on rigidly to whatever has been acquired, internally or externally, and suffer from all change. To them, their footing in apparently objective, secure 'positions' is constantly being called in question, whether the positions concerned are theoretical and 'ideological' or practical and 'useful' or ethical. So they are never free from worry and anxiety. They suffer from the contradiction between life and their own selves on the one hand and the notions they have formed of themselves and the world as it should be on the other, but know of no way to defend themselves against it other than to entrench themselves ever more wilfully, despite all contradictions, behind their own 'standpoint', to defend it, often against their better judgement, and to act according to their own 'system'. Whether thinking or acting they are always influenced by fixed ideas about reality, as it is and as it should be. In the end all that is admissible is what can be grasped and what is finished, because it 'stands complete in itself'. So they must continually classify, label, check, correct, defend, secure and try to 'do' better still, and they

*Transzendenz als Erfahrung, ed. Maria Hippius, O.W. Barth-Verlag, Weilheim, 1966.

sacrifice the fullness of life they were intended to have to the rigour of their ethical standpoint.

Perfectionism is a symptom of people trapped in a rigid I-shell. They are always annoyed that the world does not correspond to their own idea of what it should be. Full of malice at the injustice of fate or in despair at their own inadequacy, they are threatened sooner or later by nihilism, into the vortex of which even their faith in God disappears. 'There's no sense in anything.' Life runs differently and fails to correspond to their fixed idea of an all-benevolent and all-wise God. So they reject their faith. The fact that their faith was a pseudo-faith, because faith only begins, of course, where understanding as an I comes to an end, cannot be known by someone trapped in the I-circle, any more than this: that there is a Sense which is beyond sense and non-sense, and that the SENSE can only dawn when a person breaks down at the limits and at the nonsense, after all, of egocentric or merely rational explanation, and accepts this breakdown!

On the practical side of life, being imprisoned in an I-shell reveals itself in a fearful urge towards demonstrable security. Since people trapped in their I lack that original trust in life which is the expression of a Presence from the Being, nothing else remains for them but to secure themselves with the resources of their I. So their self-esteem rests exclusively on what they can do, have and know. People imprisoned in their world-I are always engaged in consolidating and safeguarding their position. They are not only constantly worried about their material security, but equally sensitive about the recognition of their person and thus concerned about their façade. Whenever they feel under attack, they stiffen or react 'badly', i.e. they contract inwardly. But they never dare to react as they feel. They suppress, out of weakness or so as not to compromise their image, the response appropriate to the wrongs of the world. Nor do they risk letting out their original impulses. So the unreleased 'charge' falls upon their hearts – and gradually breeds that existential anxiety which, unlike the fear of something definite, is the expression of 'expression' that has not been allowed, i.e. depression! And the more they shut themselves up in their shell and harden, the greater is the threat of an explosion of breakdown.

On the social side of life, people trapped in their I are both egoistic and egocentric. They cannot love. They find it difficult to put themselves in someone else's place, because basically they always revolve only round themselves. They cannot open or give themselves to another, because they always have to protect themselves, i.e. they do not feel in their self-assurance the support of the Essence. Because they lack roots in the Essence, they are afraid of losing themselves completely. Disinclined to become one with another, they also have no share in the supportive and sheltering forces of communal life. Closed to every genuine contact, they have no share in those suprapersonal forces of great Nature and the spiritual Spirit, which every genuine contact opens up for us beyond the immediate encounter.

People imprisoned in their I are closed and alien to their own depths. They are barred to their Essence and thus also to the restoring fullness, sense-giving order and unifying power from the Being alive in their Essence, superior to all orders of existence. Because they admit only what does not disturb their stubbornly held 'position', they are closed not only to the friendly forces flowing to them from the world but also to the forces of their own source and form, to the point of sterility. Because they are denied integration with the Essence-ground, they are at a standstill, undergo no change and cannot mature. And in the end not even success in the world can help them overcome their inner distress. On the contrary: success merely drives them deeper still into their blind alley; for all they manage to achieve through their own resources merely consolidates and raises still higher the wall that keeps them apart from their Essence. This explains also that apparently inexplicable fact that recognition in the world alone does not bring lasting blessings even to the 'good'; indeed, that among successful people anxiety, mistrust and emptiness often increase to the very degree to which, admired and envied by others, they make their way triumphantly in the world and 'rise'. The higher they climb the greater the danger becomes that their worldly edifice, lacking a foundation in the Essence, will collapse. There is no inner Ground independent of worldly conditions. Continuance in the world belongs only to what has roots in something Supramundane.

PEOPLE WITHOUT AN I-SHELL

To be able to live in the world, people need a *form* appropriate to themselves and to the world. In people with too much I, this form has become hardened and closed. Nothing can get in, and what is inside cannot get out. Within it such people are neither accessible to the world nor permeable for their Essence. The opposite defect is a form that is too open. Everything can get in, but nothing can stay in. People with too little I have failed to arrive at any vessel with firm walls at all. No base has been formed, nor are the walls tight. The outlines are indeterminable, and everything is open and unprotected. Lacking here are the basic conditions people need not only to exist in the world but also to accommodate their Essence in a stable way and to be able to bear witness to it in the world.

People deprived of boundaries cannot preserve their 'integrity' in face of the world. They are exposed to it without a shell. They also lack stability in face of themselves. They are at the mercy of their own drives and moods without freedom of decision. In their erratic state, their dependence on their drives and feelings, they have no constancy of purpose and no line of conduct. I-people live by a presumptuous certainty, conscious of their own arbitrary power. For people who have failed to arrive at any I, self-assertion in their existence becomes a constantly recurring problem.

In them states of complete helplessness through loss of self – for the world does what it likes with them – alternate with aggressive or defensive outbreaks of self-preservation, by which they compensate disproportionately for the impotence they feel. They also lack the power to order and shape. Their inner disorder and unformed condition is reflected in their outer state. Thus they suffer from inability to organise their life and their world. They are in constant danger of adapting themselves to such an extent that they lose themselves, and are therefore inclined to keep shutting themselves up fearfully within themselves.

They also save themselves occasionally in assumed forms and adopt mannerisms to which they cling pedantically, although these really have nothing to do with them and have no inner life. They suffer the suffering of those who are unaware of their Essence, because they lack the form which, by the way it holds the I-space in good shape, reveals the Essence.

People 'without an I' never apply themselves consciously and with determination, but live and suffer in a constant state of formless and unstable acceptance. They love and hate without moderation, for they lack a moderating identity. They also lack a considered distance. No wonder these people in particular, out of a secret fear of being at the mercy of others or of being repulsed, keep withdrawing into spasms of self-securing defensiveness – just as, conversely, I-people every now and then not only drop completely out of their rigid form but do so at the very moment when they try to thaw their frozen prison in a liberating transport of feeling. Just as people imprisoned in their I-shell are, through their hardening, in danger of sudden explosions and unexpected disintegration, so are the other people, who have too little 'armour', in danger of a sudden tensing and stiffening that is full of malice and suppressed aggression.

For people with a deficient I, their relation to the forces of the Essence and the Being striving for realisation within them is tragic. These forces irrupt in them and indeed often bring them states of profound happiness, but they cannot take root in them. What is experienced trickles away through the inability of such people to let it assume an inner form. And so they keep plunging out of the light into the dark, out of joy into profound sadness. To the outside and the inside far too open and unresisting, they are overwhelmed from inside and outside in happiness and in sorrow; but neither leaves behind any lasting or formative trace. Happiness trickles away, and misfortune bears no fruit. The people with sad eyes!

It is wrong, therefore, always to see in people's protective form only the danger of hardening. The form is from childhood on the vessel that enables people to protect the mystery of their innermost core. The shell is not only the citadel that protects people in the world, but also the shrine that guards their sacred centre. People without a shell have not developed too much I, but too little and are at the mercy of forces from outside and inside. These then invade such people with destructive power, and they cannot withstand them; or the forces shower them too richly with gifts, and they cannot hold their gift, but always come away empty-handed. If such people arrive one day at a genuine encounter with their Essence, then for the first time they sense with delight their supertemporal core. While I-people, in the Essence-experience, suddenly feel liberated and transformed into open and loving individuals, people with a deficient I really find their way in it for the first time to a form that is compact and stable, because it blossoms out of the Essence.

What has been indicated here schematically in a few words, as a contrast between two forms of I that have gone wrong, is in reality far more complicated. The 'too much' like the 'too little' is not usually equally marked in all spheres of life, but distributed over partial areas. Thus there are also people who have too much I in one respect and too little in another. These inconsistent manifestations of 'too much' and 'too little' may be due to constitutional or developmental causes, such as childhood dreams, mistakes in upbringing, ethical or religious ideologies or taboos. Neurotically fixed, they give rise to those diseases or afflictions which then prevent development in accordance with the Essence and call for psychotherapeutic treatment based on depth psychology.

THE HARMONIST

There is yet a third defective form of I, whose recalcitrance to the Essence is often overlooked because it is 'harmonious', because it brings no suffering at first and so works in accordance with the Essence: the harmonist!

Harmonists are neither hardened in a shell of suffering nor do they suffer the torments of people deprived of boundaries. They are neither tense nor relaxed, but always fit in adaptably to the given situation and always in such a way that it is pleasant for themselves and for others. They know how to shield the cosiness of their inner state resiliently against any invasion from inside or out, and, because they never give any offence in the world, they themselves also take none. But what they lack is depth. They splash away gaily on the surface but their relaxed attitude and their capacity for devotion are wanting in heart. They are lovable, but uncommitted and without love. They give themselves openly, but let nothing come too near them. They certainly give themselves, and yet live in an eternal compromise. They have a solution for everything on hand, but at little cost to themselves. They are the lovable egoists who give to all without giving themselves away, and apparently receive and accept all without putting themselves in question or at risk. They never give themselves wholly, but also leave behind no painful gap when they disappear. They look as though they are in harmony with their Essence. In fact they hardly ever come to feel it. Always adapted to the world, automatically curbing their own impulses to a harmless level, they avoid what is cold or too hot, what is really dark or too light, and in a lukewarm, half dark, half light medium they slip along on the surface of life as though without a hitch. Their faces fall into serious or cheerful folds, their voices become significantly low or hearty – entirely as the other wishes and, always 'agreeable', they are welcome guests. They appear without causing pain, and leave without losing anything. But one day for them too the moment comes when fear creeps up on them secretly. It becomes uncanny to them *how* smoothly everything is going, and they feel how superficial and empty they are, and somehow at fault. Such people must learn some time or other both to give their hearts and to engage and risk themselves. And so for this type – if their hour should ever strike – the encounter with the Essence often brings the hardest experience; for at first it is not, as for the other two, a delightful release from long suffering but, after such a long period of feeling themselves harmonious, the first real suffering, suffering from the need to forgo, for the sake of the Essence, their comfortable and practised harmonious form which has lapped them in pleasantness. But should such people once risk the jump, because even in their comfortable riding of the waves they have once felt 'sick', their experience of the Essence can blossom into a special happiness, because they can then find in it not only their real core, and through that the chance of a true form, but also a genuine lowering of barriers, and only through that the chance of true contact with the 'Thou'.

Coming of age

The distress of the man and woman of our time can be met only by someone who can help to initiate a transformation that will free them from the prison of their trapped I-world thinking and enable them to become open to a movement that signifies *coming of age*, i.e. that brings them, despite all external circumstances, to the Way of their true self-realisation, testifying outwardly to their Essence. It is a question of people who, because they have become one with their Essence, i.e. linked to the supramundane Life, and matured into Persons, have found a higher freedom, i.e. one that is independent of the world, because in them and through them the supramundane Being is at work.

'Personal maturity' presupposes more than solid knowledge and ability; it means more than moral reliability, more than confessing to a religious faith. It represents a transformation of the whole person through their being rooted in the Being in a way that has become conscious and responsibly lived. People who have attained to maturity do not know, have or do more than immature people, but they *are* more than those who have not yet matured. Human coming of age, which depends on maturity, not only brings more freedom of decision for acting in the world; it also means freedom to testify to one's own Essence and the transcendent order interwoven with it, even when freedom to act in the world is blocked. People who have come of age through being anchored in the Essence can not only do what they want (because all they now want to do is what they may), but may *be* who they *are*. They can and may be who they '*are*', would like to be and should be fundamentally, i.e. from the Essence, from God. This being-allowed-to-be in the world who one really is, i.e. according to one's Essence, is a fundamental human longing. Astir and at work in it is the heavenly origin of human beings. To come into conformity with this and be capable of testifying to it, knowing, fashioning and loving in the world of their earthly origin, constitutes the essence of *coming of age*.

What then does it mean for people to be of age?

Coming of age means taking upon oneself the yoke of that freedom in which people give up their self-will and take into their will what they have come to know in the deepest experience as the view and the concern of their supramundane Essence. Being of age means reliability in the right use of personal freedom.

People are of age who have acquired their roots in faith in experienced transcendence, as a knowledge to which they bear witness by constantly proving it afresh. Only thus do they acquire the maturity whose fruit is a life that corresponds to their destiny: to testify in this existence to the supramundane Being.

People are of age to the degree that they have become Persons who, through a binding decision in favour of the reality-content of their transcendent experience, are able and willing to obey the call heard in it to make the Being beyond space and time, which they are and perceive in their own Essence, manifest in their space-time existence. This testifying to the Being takes place with full validity only in the midst of historical existence. People who have truly come of age *are* the supramundane Being become real-in-the-world in the condition of a human being.

The supramundane Life appears in people who have come of age in the continual 'dying and becoming' of their world.

The freedom of those who have come of age means more than the mental freedom that enables people to overcome their little I and its primary drives for pleasure and power; more too than the freedom to raise themselves, by adhering to unconditioned values, above everything conditioned in the world and, in the fields of science, art and philosophy, leave the world behind them. The Essence-freedom of Persons first proves itself rather when they face up to their historical fate, accept their suffering and do not 'spiritually' ignore the unacceptable, but endure it and see it through as the gateway to another dimension.

Being of age first proves itself when threatening destruction and the contrariness of events are too much for people's natural powers, and they resist the temptation to become traitors to the Essence by turning aside or by escaping to consolation elsewhere.

Not being of age shows itself when people stick at nothing to preserve themselves, when to avoid friction they prefer a hollow truce to a showdown, when they justify an inner falsehood by an adherence to general rules that are in fact no longer valid, when they acknowledge fellowship only when it benefits or protects them, when they misuse their religious faith to hide behind a humility that is not genuine, in short whenever they decide in favour of peripheral harmony as against the disquieting forces of the depths, in favour of continuing in the 'horizontal' as against submission to the 'vertical'.

People are of age to the degree that they continually find the courage to walk through the dark places of life and by letting in, and taking seriously, the compelling stillness in which the depths call to them, are ready to see the reality of this world without a pretty veil and to let it come to them fearlessly as it is. Open to the world on the strength of their ties with the Being, they then go into every situation without dissimulation and without prejudice. They see the old and familiar with new eyes, regard themselves with suspicion whenever they imagine they have got somewhere, are on their guard against fixed ideas about the world, their fellow men and God, and, even when they have to commit themselves in the world, retain the freedom to cancel obligations in order to keep faith with their Essence, to accept the shame of being thought faithless, to give up what has been won and start again.

Those who have come of age keep faith with the Being in all the concrete relations of their historical existence by remaining oriented, throughout the changing situations, to the fundamental mission which alone is binding upon them, which speaks to them out of *all* the situations of life, without exception. Then every situation becomes 'the best of opportunities' to testify to the Supertemporal in the temporal, to the Unconditioned in the conditioned, to the Supramundane in the mundane. This is not to master the world through what is conditioned, nor to withdraw from what is conditioned, by nature or by fate, into the realms of the Unconditioned, but in the sphere of one's own responsibility in knowing and acting to let one's historical 'being-there' and 'being-thus', *in* all their conditioned state and imperfection, become transparent to the Being. But this is only possible in constant new beginnings. For the Being, the Great LIFE, which veils itself in all that has come to be and in all objective concepts, blossoms forth only in creative-redemptive new-becoming. So people are of age in whom the wheel of change never stands still, and in whom Meister Eckhart's great saying 'God's being is our becoming' is fulfilled in a 'Yes' to eternal dying and becoming.

People who have come of age testify to their roots in the Being beyond space and time, which grow from their own experience and are not merely asserted in a confession of faith, in their strength to endure what is unendurable to the natural I; to accept what is unacceptable. But that implies the strength to change oneself, stage by stage, by going through the firing-kiln again and again. Only those who are anchored in the depths of the Essence can constantly overcome the I's aversion to pain. And only for them will innocuous agreement no longer be the criterion for what is right, no longer will lack of friction be one of the highest values. Those who stand in the Supramundane become capable of putting up with the dissension and contrariness of the world without growing bitter about them but fruitful in maturity. Indeed, even more, through all the injustice and absurdity of this world there gleams for them a Sense that is beyond the sense and nonsense of this world!

People of age are not those who think they can finally overcome fear, sadness and despair, but rather those who are able to see them through and grow in the process. Of age are people for whom the distress that comes from the everlasting dangers of the world and their own imperfections always unfolds into a fresh occasion for them to recognise their immature identification with their fearful, grieving and despairing I, and on the strength of their contact with the all-nullifying Ground constantly merge with it afresh. In this way their Persons, constantly refilled and renewed by the redeeming depths and formative power of the Essence, can, *in* all their weakness, withstand, shape and master life in the world in the name of progressive transparence for transcendence.

But what gives us the right to speak in such a self-evident way of the Essence and of the supramundane Being? Experience!

III

Experience of the Being

The demand

The more peremptorily their heavenly origin, and the meaning and vocation that come to them from it as presentiment and promise, enter the inner being of the man and woman of today, pregnant with the future, the more urgent does the demand become for a precise description of the grounds that justify them in asserting any difference at all between two realities, a mundane and a Supramundane. If it is not supposed to be merely a matter of faith, whether the expression and product of wishful thinking, of a longing, or even of trust in the evidence of Holy Scriptures, then it must be possible to specify experiences – experiences of a special sort – that enable us, with the same right as that with which the experiences of our five senses allow us to assert a materially tangible world, to justify asserting the reality of another, non-worldly dimension. This assertion, however, should not be supported only by peremptory and describable experiences; it must also be possible to give criteria for the trustworthiness of such experiences. It must be possible to specify how legitimate experiences differ from such occurrences as psychic projections, the results of taking drugs, wishful images, hysterical imaginings, etc. In what follows we first give two examples of incidents in which Experiences of the Being or Contacts with the Being are involved: an exemplary childhood memory and a conversation of the kind that is being held today by the thousand.

Significant moments in life

Over the course of several sessions of psychotherapy, a woman in her mid-forties told me the story of her life. At the end of the third session I picked out an event from this story, an apparently trivial incident from her childhood. 'My dear. . . . You told me in our first session how you were once with your mother in a church . . . when the light, so you said, came through the stained-glass windows "in a strange way". As you said that your voice, it seemed to me, had a special tone. Think for a moment, was there anything special about this?'

'No,' said the woman, '– how do you mean – it was just nice . . . and yet . . . ' – and slowly what she had felt seemed to well up in her again – 'it was "nice" in a special way . . . hm, yes, it did affect me strangely at the time . . . it was very odd. . . . It only lasted a moment, but during that time it was, how shall I put it, as though I had been taken into something quite different. Yes, now I know what it was: all at once I felt so peaceful, so completely clear and warm.' She stopped and with a changed, somewhat startled expression asked hesitantly, 'Do you think I ought to take it seriously?'

'Yes,' I said, 'I do mean that, very seriously in fact, and before tomorrow think back again, and see if there haven't been other such moments in your life.'

Next day the woman came again. And when the time for it was ripe, I asked her: 'Well, have you thought of anything else?'

'Yes, Professor, I've tried to remember . . . and there were two other times in my life.' Again her look turned inwards, and then she went on: 'Once it was in a wood. I was sixteen at the time. How it came about I don't know. I had stopped for a moment. It had been raining, a ray of sunlight fell on a piece of moss – and . . . there it was again . . . exactly the same! As I looked at the moss, completely lost, it was as though I was being flooded through and through. . . . A shudder went through me, and then it was quite still inside me – and yet not in me. Then there was a sudden crack in the bushes; it caught my attention, and suddenly everything had gone.' The woman fell silent.

'And the other time?' I asked.

'Yes, I can still remember it quite clearly. It was in the tube. Sitting opposite me was an old woman. And she looked at me, that is, she actually looked right through me and yet saw me, that is, her eyes caught me right in my depths, and . . . then it was like a warm ray going into me that dissolved everything in me and joined it together again . . . . It was so good. And after it happened I had such a great force in me, as though nothing could ever happen to me again and as though everything, everything was all right.'

'And how do you think these three incidents fit together?' I asked the woman.

'Quite simply,' she said, 'it *was* after all exactly the same each time.' And all at once her face lit up and she said, in a low voice and somehow deeply moved: 'Now I know what you mean.'

From that day on the woman's life was changed. She had not only 'experienced' this Something three times, but now also recognised what had been experienced in its momentousness and real significance. She had begun to let into herself the reality which as a greater Reality permeates all our little reality everywhere, to which, however, we are usually closed, but which, if we only open ourselves to it truly, let it in and let ourselves be sustained and diffused by it, will bring about a fundamental change in our lives.

A *conversation*

'What can I do so that what I experienced at the time should come back; no, more, so that I can stay in touch with what I experienced?'

'What did you experience?'

'I don't know – I only know it was stupendous – it left me trembling all over.'

'Nice? Good?'

'Completely beyond nice or good. It was simply "That"!'

'What does that mean?'

'That, what it's all about. Stupendous, big – indescribable. Fullness – Light – Love, everything in one!'

'Quite an experience then!'

'Far more than an experience. "Experience" sounds so subjective. It was far more. It was a Presence – a presence of Who or What I don't know, a Presence that happened to me — '

'And you — '

'I was suddenly another, completely free – quite myself and in myself and at the same time united with everything. I no longer knew anything and at the same time everything, and so charged with force – and happy beyond all measure. For a moment I was completely myself; no, no longer "I" at all, and yet I was, as never before, and much, much more.'

'And what had you been doing previously?'

'Nothing. It came over me out of a clear sky, seized me, overwhelmed me, emptied me out completely, filled me up, drove me into myself, annihilated me and drew me out again – beyond myself. So it's quite unutterable.'

'And were you confused? The world about you, how was that?'

'Confused? Not at all! Clearer than I'd ever been. More than that, I saw what I'd never seen before.'

'What?'

'Into things – through them – to their very "core". Can't describe it. Everything had a quite different sense. Everything was exactly what it was and at the same time far more, something completely different, and precisely through that completely itself.'

'And you — '

'Exactly the same! Something completely different, a completely different person and precisely in that completely myself. I didn't belong to myself any more.'

'And now — '

'Ah, and now! Now I'm looking for someone who will explain it all to me. No – why explain? – confirm, who will "Take" it from me – more still, guide me. I know it lies in that direction!'

'What?'

'The meaning. Our destiny. Whatever we're here for – I need someone who understands that, who "knows" and . . .'

Thousands of such conversations are being held today. The occasion for them is always the same: an irruption of the supramundane Being into our conscious existence – frightening, promising or binding, as the case may be, at any rate momentous enough to cause those affected to take it seriously and to look for someone who can help them further.

The event that provides the occasion for such conversations can be of varying depth – only a fleeting touch, or on the other hand of great force. So it is appropriate to distinguish between Contact with the Being and Experience of the Being.

Contact with the Being

Like a silver thread, reports run through the ages of people who at some time have experienced another Reality, as though struck by lightning, which suddenly freed them from distress or, as the irruption of a promise, called them to another plane: the shattering experience of the supramundane Being irrupting into their everyday world.

But it is not always in the highly enlightening and unforgettable moments of our lives, whether shattering or blissful, that the Being, out of which at heart we live all the time, enters our inner being. There are those less prominent moments and hours in which we unexpectedly find ourselves transposed into a special state, in which, without our understanding, the Being touches us. Quite suddenly we feel strange. We are wholly present, completely there – and yet not attending to anything definite. We feel in a peculiar way 'round', 'enclosed' in ourselves, and yet at the same time open in a way in which a great fullness unfolds. We are as though suspended, and yet move safely and easily on the ground. We are as though absent and yet completely there, completely empty and full of life. We repose completely in ourselves and yet are at the same time intimately related to everything. We are removed from everything and at the same time in everything, are linked to everything and attached to nothing. We feel under inexplicable guidance and at the same time free. We feel rid of all objects and demands, are poor in the world, and yet filled from within to the brim, powerful and rich. At such moments we feel as though pervaded by something valuable which is at the same time very fragile. This is probably why instinctively we move only with caution, and take care not to stop and look too closely at what is happening to us. A primordial knowledge tells us that the warm twilight of the wakeful heart must not be disturbed here by the cold ray of our fixing consciousness, which freezes every living thing. Whenever the Being touches us, it is as though we then heard a voice from the mystics saying: 'To see as though one did not see, to hear as though one did not hear, to feel as though one did not feel, to have as though one did not have!' But the wonder fades. All at once it is gone. It is enough for us to be surprised and to ask, 'What is it?' And it vanishes. Whatever occurs, from outside or inside, to catch our attention and turn our consciousness, which just before had been like a wide dish that simply received without asking or establishing, into a ray, sharp as an arrow, that pins down what was experienced as something definite – the world, which just before had been as though enchanted and strangely interwoven with us, sinks back into its customary order. And we then stand there impoverished, on our own, faced again with the old world. What has just been felt vanishes like something dreamed. And yet it *was* no dream! It was a manifestation of the true, the actual Reality, which was able for a moment to dawn in us, because we were open and free from the shackles imposed on us by our usual consciousness. In such experiences something oversteps our usual consciousness and we experience something that is of a transcendent nature. However short this experience may be – it may last only a fraction of a second – it raises into our inner being with compelling evidence that Life which, unknown to us, runs through all our usual I-world-experience. What is really involved in this greater Life that people feel at such moments first becomes clear in the *Great* Experiences of the Being. The legitimacy of Contacts with the Being has to be understood in the light of Experience of the Being. Conversely, in the light of this understanding, the significance, for progress and work along the Way, of even the most fleeting Contact with the Being then becomes apparent.

Experience of the Being and its triune nature

One can speak of experiences of the Being as experiences of the divine Being, of transcendence, of the supramundane Life only because they differ, in the quality of what is experienced and in the effects they produce, so radically from all experiences of the world that one must set them apart from others as supramundane. It is precisely such experiences that give us the right to take discussion of our heavenly origin, and of the Kingdom that is not of this world, out of the realm of faith (which can remain untouched) into the realm of indubitable knowledge.

The fact that this knowledge does not rest upon data that can be rationally fixed and explained, but on personal experiences, the content of which eludes the objective consciousness, does not make it suspect but is, on the contrary, the necessary condition for its relevance and validity. It is no obstacle to seeing, recognising and 'holding fast' to an *order* in what are personal experiences, and in what is opened up in them.

Whenever we are touched by that dimension which certain experiences justify us in declaring to be Supramundane, it has a trinitarian character. It also appears that the trinity entering our consciousness here determines all living things and is thus the key to the understanding of everything human whatsoever. A first indication of this trinity may be given by the following incident.

Over my writing-table in Tokyo hung a Bohemian landscape by Caspar David Friedrich. A Japanese adept of Zen stood before it deeply stirred and then asked me a surprising question: 'Was he through?' 'What do you mean by "through"?' I asked in return. Without reflection the answer came in the form of a threefold question: 'Was he still afraid of death? Did he not see sense even in nonsense? Was he not governed by universal love?'

No longer to have any fear of death, to see a Sense that is beyond the sense and nonsense of this world, and to dwell in a love that no longer has anything to do with sympathy or antipathy – these are the signs of the *wise*, superior to the world. And so this Japanese could not help interpreting the transparence of the masterpiece that moved him as a sign that the painter had painted it in the state of one who was enlightened, i.e. of a person who had become one with the Reality of the Essence beyond space, time and contradictions, and so possessed that attitude to life, paradoxical from the state of the natural I, i.e. the unenlightened, in which a person no longer fears death, is free from despair at the injustice of the world and is imbued with a love that no longer depends on conditions. And the fact that this 'through' was given this threefold meaning is no accident, no private opinion, but reveals a universal structure of life in general.

We could say nothing about the Being as the supramundane LIFE that overrides and pervades all our worldly life if it did not confront us in ourselves and in all living things in three 'ways', i.e. in its trinity. And to become aware of the Being's triune nature, which in the Essence 'constitutes' us and all things, is the prerequisite and the key to all valid knowing, shaping and perfecting, of whatever or whoever it may be. In what sense are we to speak of this 'triune nature'?

Everything that lives wants to *live* and lives by a *force* that enables it to live and to offer resistance to whatever opposes life, i.e. to survive.

Everything that lives not only lives, but lives and drives towards a certain *shape*. It not only maintains itself somehow in *being-there*, but seeks a certain *being-thus*. In its shape and what is in keeping with it the living thing has its *sense*.

Everything that lives lives and perfects itself not only by the force to live and its drive to a certain shape, but by a force that testifies to *unity* and produces unity, which holds it together in itself and links it to the Whole in which it shares.

In this triune nature, which distinguishes the Life of all life in this world, the supramundane LIFE, the divine Being, which is at work in us and in all living things, manifests itself in the trinity immanent within it: as the *fullness* of the Being, which can never be exhausted; as the *order and lawfulness* of the Being as primordial image; and as the *unity* of the Being, all-embracing and at work through everything. In the fullness of the Being are grounded, in humans, their force, will and love for this corporeal life; in the quality of the Being as primordial image, the quality of the Essence as internal image, and the resulting drive of the human spirit towards a meaningful life and its perfection in a valid *shape*; and in the unity of the Being, the longing of the soul for love, for *wholeness and being-at-one*, with itself, with the world and with God.

In this triune nature of the Being – which sustains and moves all that lives – are grounded also the natural basic human concerns: to live *securely* and for as 'long' as possible, i.e. to survive; to live *meaningfully* in a structure of orders and entities in which sense, value and justice prevail; and to live in a *whole* in which human beings can experience love and are sheltered.

The basic concerns of life signify at the level of consciousness of the natural I: the will to survive, i.e. the will for a secure life; the drive towards a meaningful life, i.e. one corresponding to the person's own Essence, also a just one; and the longing for community.

The contradiction of these three basic concerns gives rise to the basic human distresses: *fear of death*, *despair at absurdity* and the *desolation of loneliness*. Human beings suffer when their life, their sense and their shelter in the world are endangered. They suffer from this 'naturally' to the degree that they are identified with their world-I and have not yet experienced themselves in their 'Essence', in which the Being, in its fullness, lawfulness and unity, is present in a way that causes what life, sense and unity are, and what is contradictory to them, to be experienced in a completely different way from when a person is in the I. Indeed, the very distresses that people experience when the basic concerns of life, understood in the I-sense, are endangered, i.e. the basic distresses of their existence, become doors to Experience of the Being and form the prerequisite and background to the 'Great Experience', the very experience of a dimension that lies beyond these 'distresses' and which frees human beings from them.

Three basic experiences

Experiences of the Being are experiences that have probably fallen to each of us at some time or other, for wwhich, however, we are usually unprepared; so we fail to recognise them for what they are and let them go again. They are blissful moments of liberation, often arising out of the greatest distress, which had driven us to the extreme. And it is precisely these 'extreme situations' that can, when a person steps over the threshold, bring an encounter with what lies 'beyond'.

Corresponding to the three basic human distresses, there are three basic experiences of the Supramundane in us, to become conscious of which suddenly frees us from worldly distress.

'In the world we are afraid . . .'; but many people have had the experience, when death was very close, as in air raids, in serious illness or in other situations where destruction threatened, of how at the very moment when their fear had reached its peak, when death was inevitable and their natural inner defences were finally collapsing, if they then submitted themselves voluntarily and, perhaps for only a fraction of a second, accepted a situation unacceptable to the natural person (and so, from the point of view of the I, which of course always wants to 'stay', did something completely paradoxical), they suddenly became quite calm, unexpectedly freed from all fear, and felt, more in fact, all at once knew, that Something was there in them and alive which no death and no destruction could come near, indeed that what in the world was called death had nothing whatever to do with it. For a moment it was clear to them: 'If I ever come out of this again, I shall know once and for all from whence and toward what I have to live.' Such people do not know *what* it is that they are encountering, or *who* they are for a moment as they have the experience, but they suddenly feel themselves different people and in a different force. They do not know from whence and do not know why. They only know: 'I stand in an indestructible force.' Here people have been touched by the Being. It has entered their inner being, i.e. the Being could become inner being because the natural I gave way and the shell cracked in which these people had set themselves up independently, and thereby at the same time, however, barred themselves against the Being.

The experience in which people encounter Something in them that lies beyond death, and so lose the fear of annihilation, is one of the experiences that cause them to speak of a supramundane Being.

The second basic distress of this life is supplied by the absurd, the downright nonsensical, when people are weighed down beyond the verge of endurable despair and are brought to the verge of madness. As, for instance, when people are treated inhumanly and cannot defend themselves, when they experience a degree of injustice that has become unendurable, when the person they are associated with or the circumstances in which they are stuck are downright nonsensical, etc. Here too something can occur that is from the natural point of view paradoxical: such people do for once what they cannot do from their usual standpoint, they accept the unacceptable. Then, as many have experienced, at the moment when they give way, say 'yes' to the nonsensical but inescapable situation, a deeper Sense dawns in them, a Sense that no longer has anything to do with the sense and nonsense of this world. All at once such people feel they are placed in an incomprehensible Order. Clarity shines through them. One cannot say clarity through what, about what, or clarity for what. It is quite inexplicable, but such people stand quite simply 'in a Supramundane clarity', as they did formerly 'in a Supramundane force'.

There is yet a third Experience of the Being of equal rank, namely when people thrown into utter loneliness – through the loss perhaps of their closest companion, through being expelled from their community, or something similar – fall into a sadness that exceeds the possible degree, for them, of endurable desolation. If it is then granted to them to do what cannot be done and submit themselves, if only for a moment, to reality as it is, thus once again accepting the unacceptable, then it *can* happen that they will suddenly feel caught up as though by invisible arms, embraced in a Love and sheltered in a Mystery of which they could not say who loved them or whom they loved. They simply find themselves, as formerly in a state of force or a state of clarity, so now sheltered in a Supramundane love and have become thereby an all-absorbing, all-annulling supramundane Being, which has dawned in them and which overrides all their previous ideas of existence.

Three kinds of self-awareness

The triune nature of the Being pressing for manifestation in us is an *a priori* human experience. For, whether we are aware of it or not, we experience ourselves and the world always and everywhere in this threefold aspect. So too in our self-awareness. In accordance with the triune nature of the Being becoming conscious in us there are three forms of self-awareness. The Being as fullness of life appears as self-*force*-awareness, the Being as law appears in us as self-*value*-awareness, and the Being as all-connecting unity appears as self-*we*-awareness. But self-awareness always means something different according to whether people are still rooted solely in the world-conditioned and world-related

I, and thus have only an I-world-self, or in the unconditioned Essence superior to the world, and thus have a self grounded in the Essence, i.e. are present to themselves only in their earthly origin or also in their heavenly origin, which may have dawned in them in experience of the Being.

If people are grounded only in their world-I, then their self-force-awareness depends on what they have, know and can do; a self-force-awareness grounded in what they are. This proves itself therefore precisely when, from the point of view of the world, there is nothing any more that they have, know or can do; it is precisely when they are threatened with destruction that they feel themselves firmly grounded in another Life, indestructibly in what they *are*. This can be the gift of a Great Experience.

The self-value-awareness of the world-I depends on assessment by others. A self-value-awareness grounded in the Essence is completely independent of that. Indeed, it is experienced precisely when the world rejects people, does not understand them or scorns them. It is the basis of a royal independence.

The self-we-awareness of the world-I depends on the presence of secure contacts, actual ties with a 'thou', and shelter in a community. Shelter in a 'we' grounded in the Essence, i.e. true self-we-awareness, is experienced precisely in moments of exclusion from the world, in the desolation of being left alone, in loneliness. It is precisely against the background of being alone in the world that people grounded in the Essence feel that they belong to a sheltering, supramundane Whole, suffused with love. This too can be the permanent gift of a Great Experience.

Power, wisdom and goodness

Experience of the Being is the experience of a dimension in which space-time existence, with all its distress, is overtaken and overcome. People experience themselves in their Essence and in that feel themselves to be in a Supramundane force, a never-suspected *power*, in the clarity of a *wisdom* which removes questions about sense to a completely different plane, and at the same time in a love which at once radiates in a *goodness* which, whatever it may embrace, is completely independent of conditions, of sympathy or antipathy, of good or evil. Supramundane power, wisdom and goodness: are these not – as all who have experienced the three in themselves can discover with almost frightening surprise – the three great 'attributes' which all religions ascribe to their gods?

Certainly, but to say such a thing is a subjectivisation or psychologisation of the Divine, is it not, or a dangerous hubris that is raising its head here? It is neither! It is the expression of an experience that in our Essence we share in the Divine itself. So long as human beings remain spellbound within the all-too-human limits of their I-centred, objective consciousness, and in the ontological concept of reality arising from it, in whose ambit nothing that is experienced non-objectively – nothing either pre-objective or supra-objective, as it is actually experienced – can enter or find a place, the assertion that at heart they themselves have a share in the Divine will naturally appear to them hubristic. This sharing in the divine Being, however, is the very thing that must be recognised and accepted; it is then not a sign of hubris, but of genuine *humility*.

Humility has two sides: the one that is familiar to us all implies 'Not to want to appear more than one is!' The other, however, usually forgotten, implies 'Not to want to be less than one is!' The meaning of the Great Message and of the deepest human experience is utterly distorted by the view and the assertion that identifies people with their I, which sets itself off from the Being, and from that declares them to be altogether remote from God and ungodlike to their very foundation, instead of allowing them the divinity of their Essence and with that the royal element in their humanity as a basic characteristic. It is the mistaken assumption of those without experience that experience of our divine Essence makes us 'hubristic'. On the contrary, it is the very thing that makes us feel and recognise the infinite distance between what each of us has become under the conditions of the world and what one is, and should become entirely, as someone who is marked by the Essence. But no defective form of I-growth, in which people remote from the Being strive wilfully after property, prestige and power, can rob them of their core. So there is a genuine feeling of guilt and a consciousness of sin, not only towards the world and towards human beings, but still more from the failure to be true to this core.

Thus consciousness of sin and feeling of guilt can characterise the human image only when those responsible for developing the image lack experience of the Being, set the world-I in place of the Essence and dare not admit the Essence, even if they should happen to experience it, from fear of hubris.

We must get away from the misleading tradition which, from fear of the danger of vain *superbia*, avoids proud self-awareness of an Essence that is royal at heart, and which sees human beings theoretically in a false anthropology that virtually confines them in feelings of inferiority because it is too narrow. Thus even people who, grown up in the negative tradition, have *had* the Great Experience, and who have known themselves in it as quite different people, are now reluctant to admit to themselves that with it and through it they have acquired a human *rank* that is higher than that of people who have not had the experience, or have not been transformed by it. A higher rank? Is *that* not hubristic? Only if the people who experienced the Being add the 'more' which they now have to their world-I, and give that the credit for it, are they hubristic. If, however, they dare to grant themselves their now *being*-more as a Person as a gift from the Essence, they will manage what has fallen to them properly and in particular be in a position to help others to find it who are seeking it in themselves. People become sinful who live in disregard of what they are from God in the Essence and will not admit it, when they experience it, not those who accept it happily and try to carry out self-responsibly as a mission what they have experienced as a promise, as a promise that is inherent in us all as children and citizens of the Kingdom that is not of this world.

Two forces work in human beings against each other: the drive of the Essence to become manifest in the world, and the arbitrariness of the I which, in its will to endure and its value-consciousness, its aversion to pain and its need for pleasure, sets itself against the will of the Essence. So the breakthrough to the Essence in Experience of the Being can also have two faces: liberation from the threefold distress, which first comes to human beings, indeed, from their being I-centred; for it is from that, of course, that humans suffer fear, despair and desolation in and at the world. On the other hand, however, the breakthrough to the Essence can also be quite simply and without immediate distress the shining experience from the Essence of the promise inherent in us in the Essence. Hours of grace, of experience of the grace inborn in us, in and with our Essence! Moments of all-embracing transformation! Suddenly, quite without cause, one feels like a different person, and everything in the vicinity, people and objects, are bathed in a different light and shine from a different core!

It is important to be aware of these two possibilities: Experience of the Being as the turning-point of some distress and Experience of the Being in which, groundlessly as it were, quite simply as a gift, the Essence enters one's inner being, shining like a ray from another world that makes everything glow in a new light. The quite unforeseen irruption is already present, of course, in Contact with the Being – which allows us all at once, quite without distress, to feel the breath of the Being. If one looks more closely, however, one will find that such surprise Contacts with the Being have usually been preceded by some passage through suffering, in which the people concerned had forfeited a bit of their well-guarded I-property, days in which they had almost cracked at something unacceptable, nights of tears, of grief or suffering from some absurdity or wrong of this world. Before virtue the gods have set sweat;

before the entrance to their Kingdom, the surrender of the 'kingdom' of
the citizen of this world.

Criteria for a genuine experience of the Being

Experience of the Being is experience of a Reality that oversteps the
natural I and its powers of comprehension, which is indeed even
paradoxical to it. This experience takes the supernatural Reality that
opens up in it out of the realm of mere faith and adds it to human
knowledge as a special knowledge. Such experiences are more frequent
than is generally known. But only people who have reached a certain
stage are attuned to them and feel themselves basically at home in, and
bound by, the Reality that opens up in them. What is it, however, that
provides the certainty that valid knowledge is really gained here and that
a person has not been the victim of an illusion, of a projection of
subjective desires and hopes? What are the criteria by which it can be
known that such experiences really are experiences of another dimension, hence valid experiences of the Being? There are five of them:

1 the unmistakable character of their quality;
2 the special radiation that accompanies them;
3 the transformation that takes place;
4 the birth of a new conscience;
5 the emergence of the Adversary.

THE QUALITY OF THE NUMINOUS

Part of every Experience of the Being, and indeed of every Contact with
the Being, is the specific quality of the experience, the *numinous*. The
numinous is the quality of the experience which always, and however
gently, causes the presence of the LIFE at work through everything to be
felt through the veil of the immediate facts and whatever dominates the
foreground of consciousness. It touches us and embraces us as an aura
that affects us strangely, which brings into our inner being, through the
wall of the factual world with its hard outlines, something which
overrides the factual world and yet also speaks within it out of the
Essence of all things. To the extent to which people dwell on things that
are known, to which they fix world-reality, in detail or in its larger
connections, and move within its orders, the ever-unfixable vibration-
reality of LIFE will lie outside their ken. In other words, the miraculous
force of the Wholeness of LIFE present in all things, which at heart

continually widens people, keeps them alive, inspires and renews them, will not come into their inner being. But precisely because the Presence of this all-embracing Whole constitutes, in the form and language of a person's individuality, the true core of every human being, it can, if it has been condemned to the shadows for too long, appear one day, rebelling and liberating, in the light of consciousness and illumine all things afresh.

The numinous is the quality that indicates, infallibly and unmistakably, the Presence of another Reality in human consciousness. No word is adequate to describe it. It cannot be classified in any way. It shatters the limits of every word, every concept, every image; it is not the superlative of a special sense of the beautiful, for instance, or of the good. It is something quite different, which can be associated with any worldly feeling, mood, quality, with any content whatsoever – on one condition: that these are transparent for precisely this indescribable something-quite-different, which touches us in the quality of the numinous.

The numinous runs through the content of every religious experience. We have no term for it in English. The word 'holy' does not quite meet the case. Everything holy may well be numinous, but not everything numinous is holy. In French there are two words – 'saint' and 'sacré', the sanctum and the sacrum. We would have to say the holy and the sacred. In our tradition holy is associated with a person – the Person of God, Christ, the holy Mother of God, the Holy Ghost or the saints. It now seems as though the retreat of the man and woman of our time from traditional religion, and so from the presence of holy persons, has made them shy away from admitting the numinous at all, or even the sacred. We must re-establish open-mindedness with respect to experience of the numinous; indeed, more still, we must give it the rank due to it in the hierarchy of qualities that can be experienced.

The concept of the numinous includes something more than the sacred. It echoes with the ambivalence of the transcendent, hence also the dark transcendence. The gruesome, the eerie, the ghostly, the satanic also have a numinous quality.

The quality of the numinous can adhere to anything. It can be experienced in nature, in an encounter with a person, in dancing, in eroticism, in art (e.g. at certain moments when the word 'beautiful' is no longer sufficient). What touches us here, as R. Otto has shown for the holy, is always at the same time a *tremendum* and a *fascinosum*. It is something that, as C. G. Jung says, 'overwhelms' us, that lifts us or lures us, with the powers of the attractive as well as those of the dangerous, beyond the customary space of our world-I into another dimension that transcends our I-horizon, where something awaits us that can destroy or save, captivate or liberate. In every case, however, what touches us in the numinous carries us somehow beyond ourselves.

The eerie ambivalence of the numinous runs through the realm of the Masters, the proclaimers and mediators of promised blessings, but also that of the destroyers of all that stands in their way. Danger is in the air, the danger of being destroyed as the old I; but for that very reason the air is also full of the promise of a new Being. And so the initiatory Way, designed to lead to the numinous, is always surrounded uncannily by danger and by promise.

The numinous is one of the basic qualities of childlike experience. In infancy life is still unbroken and unfragmented, still present as an undivided Whole. When the objective consciousness and its centre, the I, conscious of itself and its world, begins to awaken and to grow, the Unity, which still after all supports, inspires and shelters life, can evoke in the fringe of consciousness that quality of experience which then lives on and is remembered later by many people as the 'radiance of childhood'. So long as the objectively rational consciousness, which creates matters-of-(f)act, fixes in concepts and orients itself by their classification, is still undeveloped, the whole of experience is still shot through with something wondrously comprehensive, as it always is after all among 'primitives'. The further development of the objective, fact-creating, rational consciousness is then accompanied by the loss of that feeling which may be remembered later as the magic of childhood. But, when the lightning of consciousness strikes, which suddenly transforms the environment into a world that gives an answer to the factual question 'What is that?', fixes what is experienced and gives it a name, i.e. creates matters-of-fact, something else can come to flower which, as the field of discovery, can *itself* have a numinous radiance. So children then experience two wonders alternately: against the background of the as yet undifferentiated Whole the wonder of the 'world', which gradually comes into being objectively, in parallel to their I, with the magic of all the things – Oh, wonder! – that it contains; and on the other hand, against the background of the world that is constituting itself materially as a multiplicity of facts, children still experience 'intrinsically' the wondrous nature also of the encompassing Whole, in the numinous quality of an aura that pervades all their experience.

THE RADIATION

People who are touched by the Being and are open to It, especially those who have just had an Experience of the Being, but also those who are still borne along by its after-effects, have a special radiation.

In the radiation a force appears which oversteps the horizon of our usual consciousness. The halo is not an invention of pious artists. That people of great permeability possess a radiation which can intensify into actual manifestations of light is a well attested fact. That a special eye is needed to see it no more robs it of its reality than any other quality of the senses is robbed of its reality by the fact that something is needed to perceive it for it to exist at all. But the sense that enables us to perceive this special quality of light can be developed. For the work along the Way it is important, however, to learn to recognise the difference between the radiations of a shallow light that has its origin in worldly conditions, in the joys and sorrows of this world, and the other radiations, whose source makes it possible to recognise that they are touched or imbued with the breath of the other dimension.

That the light which has a transcendent origin lies beyond our usual visual capacity, just as certain frequencies of vibration are beyond our normal powers of hearing, is certain. But to perceive this light requires not only a quantitative increase in our usual powers of perception, but the development of a qualitatively different perceptive potential. Where this potential has been cultivated it represents a different stage of consciousness. There are people who are blind or deaf to the Being. So too are there those who can or cannot perceive such radiation, in others and in themselves. There are very intelligent people who are deaf to the Being, and there are rationally underdeveloped people of great sensitivity to the Being. Refinement of the soul is something different from sharpness of mind.

Just as the numinous quality is not the superlative of some customary quality of feeling, so is the radiated light from the Being not an optical phenomenon in the usual sense. It is an aura which, by testifying to the presence of another dimension, indicates at the same time a certain stage in people and, for it to be perceived, presupposes also a certain permeability. For those who are able to detect this aura the 'air' in the presence of people permeated by the Being is changed. The total atmosphere as light and colour, as tonal quality, as smell and as a medium that can be felt as it were in a tactile way, has a special character and is in a special way transparent. Conversely, the air round very material people i.e. their aura, is impermeable, somehow pasty, often stuffy and somewhat grimy, toneless, without vibration, spiritually empty, without inspiring force and – for all its occasional, even juicy, fullness – without depth.

The radiation is something different from an 'emanation' or even a 'shine'.

There is the delightful radiation that emanates from a young person, such as the radiation from a young girl, who as yet knows nothing of malice and steps out pure and unconstrained. But this forward-looking fullness of life, of a life that is present at first only as promise, is all that constitutes this sort of radiation. The 'shine' is strongest when the establishing consciousness begins to weave a veil of ignorance about the onlooking soul, and when now, in the approaching obscuration, the Being begins to shine in a special way. When worldly knowledge consolidates itself and all that is experienced turns into a firm-standing order of objects, the light from the Essence pales; for in a 'comprehended' existence the Being is obstructed and hidden and the grown-ups, lost in the objectively conceived world, usually live their lives as people who have grown away from the Being-light. In the daylight of their world-consciousness the light of their Essence-star has paled.

All things and all creatures have their emanation, hence plants, flowers, trees, stones, all objects and also human beings. Such an emanation is rather like the giving-off of a subtle material substance. Its character depends in each case on conditions. So too does the atmosphere that emanates from anything material. In this sense all things, all creatures and places have each their particular emanation. Thus the living have a different one from the dead, the old a different one from the new, the sick a different one from the healthy. Each colour too has its own particular emanation. And connected with this in each case is the general feeling or mood, even the feel of a room, a comfortable living-room in contrast to a laboratory. People vary in their sensitivity to these multifarious kinds of 'emanation'.

The radiation that accompanies transparence for the 'Essence', which is present in Contact with the Being or in Experience of the Being, is something special. In it the LIFE itself touches us in a language that is always different and yet with a tone that is always the same. This always has the character of a special purity, freshness and depth. It is as though the eternal youth of the Being makes itself felt here, to which transparence provides a window. Probably the most moving example of this is the process of transfiguration in the face of someone who has just died. A glowing occurs, like the reflected glory of infinity. The radiance of the Essence shines forth. And then the shocking transition to being really dead, to a corpse. The deceased crumples, shrinks and sinks into itself (the corpse is no longer the person). The transparence is gone, and lying there, waxy and stiff, like something obnoxious, is a lifeless body that no longer answers either inwardly or outwardly. And, as it decays, it gives off the smell of putrefaction. The transfiguration is the expression of a Presence of the Being, which, thanks to the full transparence that occurs at death, can be experienced directly.

The radiation in which the Being speaks cannot be localised; it is beyond anything concrete. So naturally it cannot be perceived with the consciousness that establishes and holds fast. Thus people trapped in the rational consciousness, such as doctors, who simply establish the fact of death, do not 'see' the transfiguration – they speak perhaps of 'relaxed features', of a 'peaceful expression'. With that they are stuck on the surface of the finite and the conditioned. The depth of the Being, pre-existing and exempt from everything conditioned, the Majesty of the Divine, which here becomes an event, is closed to them. The radiation of the Being dawns in us only in the encounter of Essence with Essence. So whenever it touches us we feel ourselves touched in our core, addressed and called in our true Essence, called and present.

There is also, however, the dark radiation. This is something different from the negative emanation from the people who are unhappy, angry or in a bad mood, or obsessed by fear and unfriendly. There is a dark radiation of a transcendent character. This is something sinister, as where something evil, something destructive of a supramundane character, is in the air, something downright diabolical, which takes pleasure in devastation, an out-sized, sardonically-grinning 'No' that pours scorn on everything that is Light, as force, meaning or love. This destructive radiation can exist among people, things or places which are occupied by dark powers.

Along the initiatory Way it is important to develop one's faculties for negative radiation, which indicates negative transcendence, just as much as for positive. People who are on the Way must learn to recognise above all their affinity for negative transcendence. The secret attraction of evil. The Adversary *in* us, that principle which fundamentally calls in question or destroys Life in its triune nature as force, meaning and unity. Human beings *have* the Devil in their bodies. Only when they become aware of this will they have the strength to desire what is evil but do what is good! Those with a spiritual calling will also experience the negative transcendence of the uroboreal, the lure of the 'Great Mother', which is a threat to the spirit.

There is also, however, a false 'shine', which emanates not from the Essence but from the I, which has put itself seductively in its place. This false shine comes from a Lucifer-glittering light that dazzles but does not illuminate. Its shine is often very similar to true radiation. And yet it is something fundamentally different. The sure discrimination of the true from the Luciferan light presupposes a Presence from the Essence. People who are still occupied by their world-I are easily led astray by the false light, for this always has about it something that is attractive and fascinating to the world-I. But it is a cold light. There is no heart in it. It flashes at one like a promise. But it is a delusion. It is mendacious, shallow and has nothing behind it.

One finds the false shine among people who were originally born perhaps to be in a special way bearers of the Essence-light. But because they have put themselves in place of the Being looking out, It cannot get through. The area between them and their Essence has not been cleared. It is blocked by their I, self-assertive, in need of prestige and avid for power. So people like this remain unfulfilled, and their 'shining' look has something probing and at the same time predatory. Through the apparent fullness we feel poverty and emptiness, through the simulated closeness and warmth, a non-committal, cold distance and the chill of a bleak isolation, and through the trust-demanding forcefulness, a deadly danger, the murderer in the guise of a friend. And in spite of all this such people with the iridescent look, with their flashing teeth and winning gestures, but above all with their false smile, are often born seducers.

THE TRANSFORMATION

What greater proof could there be of the reality of an 'experience' than that it transforms people to their very depths, makes them suddenly see the world differently and decides them to start a new life and enables this to be fundamentally different from the one lived previously?

What in the world of suffering humanity could better deserve the title 'real' than that which transforms a person from one who was afraid to one who no longer fears death; from one who had fallen into despair at the senselessness and injustice of the world to one who through all absurdity is conscious of a higher Sense; and from one who was going to pieces in the desolation of his or her loneliness to one who *in* it experiences the Great Shelter? How can something that brings about such a transformation, to a supernatural attitude, perception and experience, be denied the character of reality, a Reality in fact of a Supramundane kind?

The other dimension, the transcendent Reality, appears in life not only as deliverer from distress – the supramundane fullness and force that liberates us from fear of annihilation, the supramundane Sense that saves us from despair at the absurd, the all-connecting Unity that frees us from the desolation of utter loneliness. It appears also as the Reality whose emergence 'upsets' in every respect those who live only as a world-I and are satisfied with their sensual regime and system of values! What seemed to such people to stand firm and give them security turns out basically to be 'built on sand'; what seemed in the foreground so meaningful now fails to meet the test, appears as basically inessential; and their shelter in a community or their ties with other people are put to the question, whether they do not in truth obscure the Essence and counterfeit as fulfilment what is basically a flight from their most primary mission.

For people caught by the Being their whole conception of life is overthrown. A good conscience turns out to be a façade behind which are concealed anxiety, falsehood and guilt. The values above all which such people (not only egoists) pursued with the best intentions are called in question by the Essence, not only because fixed positions are in any case a contradiction to it and are now inevitably included in the dying away of all that has come to be, but because they neglected perhaps the basic longing of the Being, and failed to allow it to become manifest in the world in its triune nature, in constant change.

People *must* stand up to life with their resources, give it meaning and have and support their community. But to the very degree that they seek to settle and secure themselves in it in a definite form they will come to feel sooner or later, the moment they open themselves to the Being, how harsh are its all-upsetting demands. For a Christian the decisive criterion for the reality of what dawns in Experience of the Being is not so much the experience of being redeemed from the distress of this world as of being called to 'follow', i.e. to an active opening of ourselves to the 'Kingdom that is not of this world', which is inherent in us. In the world he was afraid; by giving up his world-I, by accepting annihilation, by taking death upon himself, he experiences a Kingdom in which there is no death. By taking upon himself the absurd, the anguish of the greatest injustice and non-sense, i.e. by accepting what is unacceptable to the world-I, by letting darkness come upon him, the Light that is not of this world dawns in him. And finally, when he had undergone loneliness, the last unlivable loneliness, he experiences redemption in being taken home into the supramundane Unity, the love of the Being. However a believing Christian may interpret the redemption of mankind from sin through the suffering and death of Jesus Christ, one way to understand it arises, therefore, from taking *seriously* the sayings: 'My Kingdom is not of this world', 'Ye are my brethren', 'I have given ye an example'. When people follow Christ's example by accepting the unacceptable, they *experience* this Kingdom, experience through a concrete *imitatio Christi* their redemption from the consequences of their separation. They have then received the grace inborn in them – 'that which they are in the core of their being' – and, in renouncing all the demands of the world-I for survival, meaning and security, they have experienced the bliss of their Essence, sheltered in the Supramundane, in which they never were unredeemed!

A different question is how long people can keep this feeling of redemption that falls to their lot in an Experience of the Being. A different question still is now far this interpretation of 'redemption through Christ' bypasses that of traditional theology. Insofar as the latter has in mind only the 'natural' person on the one hand and on the other wants to see only the *miraculous*, there is no bridge between the two interpretations. But insofar as theology too acknowledges the 'core' of human beings to be something that points beyond them, as the 'Word' inborn in them, it would not make sense to exclude the transforming *experience* of this Word from the possibilities of being human. If it is admitted, then a bridge is built for the understanding of what has been given to mankind through Christ, a bridge whose availability is crucial to a generation that is looking for the religious foundations of its life, but which will have nothing to do with 'miracles' in the sense of the world-I. In Experience of the Being the opposition between the man and woman of reason and the believer in miracles is resolved.

THE BIRTH OF A NEW CONSCIENCE

Every genuine Experience of the Being contains the blissful feeling of being released from the confinement and distress of all the limitations of the world and with that something of the happiness of an unsuspected fullness, and infinite Sense and a Supramundane shelter. But such an Experience of the Being is really 'genuine' only when it is accompanied by the birth, or renewal, of the Essence-conscience – and so not only means release, but also imposes inalienably a commitment and prepares people, or restores them, for a new life, the pervading and determining sense of which from then on is above all the 'inner Way'. What is meant is the Way of transformation to a disposition thanks to which such people become ever more capable of testifying to, and serving, what they have encountered for a moment in Experience of the Being as the source of strength, meaning and authority! It is commitment to the initiatory Way. The conscience awakening here is the absolute conscience.

There are three kinds of conscience: the first, *childlike conscience*, comes from *fear of punishment*. This kind of conscience has greater weight than is generally suspected. The fear of hell, or even of the consequences of a bad or false life, is part of it, the 'karmic conscience'.

The second conscience is heard as the *voice of the whole* to which one belongs as a member. 'The "is" of the whole is the "must" of its members'.* Unquestionable oneness with a person, a community, a business, an idea, a work, existing ties and obligations, appears in 'pangs of conscience' the moment one does not act automatically in its spirit, fails in respect of it or becomes 'disloyal'. 'Loyalty is the essence of honour' (Hindenburg). If one becomes disloyal one loses one's honour, and that means losing one's existence, i.e. one's 'identity' as a member of the circle whose precondition and criterion of membership is the loyalty of its members.

The third conscience is the *absolute conscience*. It is experienced when a higher Authority forces a person to do something that the first conscience puts behind it, and which the second conscience also rules out, by requiring if necessary disloyalty, betrayal or disgrace. Raising itself peremptorily in this conscience is the demand of the Essence, which annuls all the ties and commitments of this world – 'let the dead bury the

* *Psychologie der Gemeinschaft, Neue Psychologische Studien*, 1926.

dead'. And this conscience is raised to full awareness in Experience of the Being, just as, conversely, when it lays hold of a person, it is itself evidence of the presence of the Being.

Obedience to the absolute conscience does not involve the old conflict between inclination and duty; it is a duty that arises through an 'inclination of our Essence' against inclination *and* duty in and towards the world! The experience and strengthening of this conscience is an inalienable part of the 'initiatory Way'.

THE EMERGENCE OF THE ADVERSARY

It is a strange thing that Experience of the Being infallibly brings the Adversary on to the scene. Whenever the Essence appears, the anti-world crops up. The Adversary is a power that hinders or destroys the Life intended by God. The more unequivocally and unconditionally people find their way to the Supramundane and enter its service, so much more certainly is the Adversary on the spot and trying to divert them from the right Way. This is no pious tale, but a fact of experience, which cannot be accounted for psychologically. If a person is blessed with an Experience of the Being, then twenty-four hours will not go by without something happening to him or her which will mar the blessings of the frame of mind the Experience had brought them to in a liberating and committing way. This happens to them from the outside, not as a psychological compensation, which by a law of balance sometimes causes an exuberant happiness to turn abruptly into a mood of depression, or a feeling of grief into an outwardly groundless cheerfulness. The blow comes from outside: an attack, an insult, some painful news, an accident – added to which there is always the fatal temptation to talk. 'Those with full hearts have overflowing mouths.' Which is unfortunate; for even the joyful Mystery lives by being guarded. If one breaks silence and lets it out, its blessing is gone.

A world-wide example of the Adversary's game is drugs. It is no accident that at the moment – not before – when for the first time along a broad front, including young people above all, Western men and women are becoming open to Experience of the Being, the Adversary turns up and holds out drugs to them – 'Look, you can have it far more easily, the beautiful experience; a bit of this stuff and you won't need to try any more; you'll have it.' And young people are snared by the temptation to arrive at beautiful experiences without effort and to put this in place of an inner work, i.e. an effort which, in a legitimate way, in a process of transformation, makes possible what the drug-experience promises to supply in an illegitimate way without any effort: an expansion of one's usual world-consciousness into the ability to experience the Supra-mundane in its redemptive and creative fullness.

Transparence

Every Experience of the Being means change – change as a momentary event and change as mission. The change set off by and imposed in Experience of the Being is aimed at the Great *Permeability*, at *Transparence* for the *Transcendence* inherent in human beings. Transparence means the frame of mind in which people are able to perceive the supramundane Being inherent in their Essence and to let it become manifest in them and through them in their world. In this transparence human beings first really become *Persons*.

The Being as all-animating force, shaping power and Light appears in the state of transparence, in its triune nature of life-engendering fullness, its quality as internal image and its unity, now more in one, now more in another aspect.

In all three ways the shining of the Being touches us differently, according to our stage of maturity. But the Being becomes truly perceptible, tangible in an intangible way, only in the to and fro of the three ways in which it manifests itself to the human sense. This sense open to the Being is itself, however, a way of the self-manifesting Being. To a purely worldly sense the Supramundane remains closed for ever. And so the perception of the Being in the trinity of its ways, possible only for mankind, is not to be seen as a purely human way, but so to speak as a self-encounter of the Being in the human consciousness. In this self-encounter the Being manifests itself in a human way and has in that, for people whose own selves have become entangled or lost in the autonomous life of their objective consciousness, a redemptive and creative character.

When the Being enters one's inner being as fullness, the state of transparence is experienced as a force from the presence of the Being sparkling in its creative potency. People encountering it feel as it were the divine *élan vital*, feel in the exuberance of the life pressing within them not only the renewing but also the shaping-creative formulae of life, the preserving and renewing forces of the depths. They experience all this like an infinite potential which, pressing into their inner being, almost shatters it. And in a genuine Experience of the Being they go through all this quite independently of their position in the world. Indeed, it is the very mark of the Great Transparence that the experience of the Being giving itself in it is completely independent of any equivalence in our existence conditioned by space and time. The fullness of the Being is experienced as power, richness and force precisely in conditions of great poverty, impotence and weakness. And so too in its quality as significant internal image the Being wells up precisely in the desperate absurdity of the world, and as all-pervading, sheltering Unity enters the inner being precisely in the state of greatest abandonment and loneliness. Thus genuine transparence signifies the overcoming of the world in the midst of its dangerousness, absurdity and cruelty and in their corresponding states of fear, despair and sadness. Indeed, transparence for the supramundane Life is, as it were, the child of death in the little life and its vehicle, the little I. That is so during life and completely so in physical death, when for human beings the glory of a greater Life falls due.

Experience of the Being is the star about which the religious life of all religions revolves. Whatever its name may be or whatever the particular notions may be that are associated with it, according to the canon of its spiritual and clerical tradition, at heart, in its varying depth, persistence and colouring it is always the same – whether it is called Satori, Samadhi or Praesentia Dei. And always and everywhere it occurs as a passing event or as a happening that marks a person once and for all with a new character: it occurs as a passing state or as a persistent feeling lasting hours, even days. And it occurs – according to readiness, stage and degree of maturity – as a quickly-passing opening of the eyes out of the sleep of objective consciousness or as a final awakening to new sight. But an enlightenment, whether unique or repeated, of short or long duration, does not make an enlightened person, nor a state of grace a person transformed by grace. So a distinction must be made between encounter and transformation, between the initiatory experience and the initiatory Way, which prepares for this experience, revolves about this experience and accepts what is experienced in it as a mission for transformation.

IV

The Way

Experience of the Being
and transformation

When experience of a supernatural Being comes to people, it can represent a transforming event which turns the meaning of life through a hundred and eighty degrees. When the axis of life breaks through from the middle of natural human existence to a new Ground of life, which is experienced against the background of existence in the natural world as a supernatural, divine Being, people are marked by a new mission. Yet only when such people are able to take the experience deeply in earnest and let it catch hold in them, so that it becomes the impulse for a new life, will they arrive at the Way. In the Supernatural they have experienced there they know themselves from then on to be supported and nourished, shaped and called, directed and sheltered by a LIFE that embraces them and constitutes in the ground of their Essence a part of their own selves!

Genuine experience of the Being is first proved and fulfilled in people's obedience to the call to transform themselves now truly into what they experienced for a moment *in* the experience. Such people then feel themselves and their world determined progressively by a Reality that not only fills them with happiness as supernatural Being but takes them strictly into its service. Blissful but at the same time filled with a new responsibility, they then know all at once that they are destined and called to open up and transform the world and themselves radically from out of this Being, knowing, loving and shaping in a deeper sense. Their lives no longer stand in the tension between the lures and demands of the world and fear or obedience in regard to a distant God – but on the Way to the progressive release of the divine force, inherent in them and now unfolding in them, which not only delivers them again and again from the distresses of this existence, but makes them *creative* for the *transformation* intended by God of the world whose author He is.

Becoming one with the Being as an experience, the experience of our heavenly origin in a significant moment of our existence, is only the possible beginning and starting-point of a Way to human transformation, the purpose of which is transparence, the progressive permeability of the whole person for the Being present in his or her Essence. The meaning of the Great Experience, in which the I ceases to exist, is not its total dissolution, but its transformation. Transformation to transparence is the task of the inner Way. Along it the person must learn to do justice progressively, in the midst of the 'outside', to the 'inside', not only of him- or herself but of all things.

When Being and Essence are perceived only in opposition to the world-related and world-conditioned I people are still under the spell of their natural world-I, whose consciousness perceives everything in opposites and so, quite naively, distinguishes the Being and the world as two Somethings, perceives them in opposition to each other and causes them to be felt as mutually antagonistic. But the true fruit of people's becoming one with their Essence is a new existential mode of being, in which the supra-objective Being and Essence and an equivalent consciousness determine life, giving it an authority and a centre in such a way that even the natural consciousness, still present, is aware of its position as 'profane' in the forecourt of the temple, in the service of which it must now prove itself, preparing and digesting experience.

The subduing of the consciousness that creates opposition between world and Essence comes about only as the fruit of a long process of growth. It is only when people truly mature into Persons that the space-time world and the supra-world become integrated, so that the world-I becomes ever more transparent for the Essence and the Essence becomes progressively more able to shine through in the world-I. In the Complete Person, who takes in both poles, the transparent and that which shines through then coincide increasingly, and people who experience this can say of themselves: 'The eye that sees me and the eye with which I see is one eye.' Then, by virtue of our transparence, the transcendence inherent in us has become manifest to itself in our humanity.

In human beings self-realisation does not take place as in plants of its own accord. It is the collaborative answer to the summons: 'I have called thee by thy name, for thou are mine.' The summons that is heard in experience of the Being, to human beings in their uniqueness, hence intended quite personally and individually, committing them to a new life, is to be clearly distinguished from the calling-home that it also contains. People who have lost their way in the world must come home to their Father's house. To stay there and efface themselves as individuals? That would be the Eastern way. In the Western, however, and Christian, as we believe, people lose in this going-home only their vagrant I, in order to generate now as witness as to the Father a new I, which will again go out into the world – as an individual Person, through whom the call of the Being resounds, world-redeeming and creative.

But who know their own name? The form given over to human beings does not simply accrue to them. They must first discover themselves in the Essence and the Way to self-realisation given over to them from the Essence. This realisation then needs their responsible co-operation. Without that they will not acquire the form intended for them; but, without an ever-deepening experience of the Being, their own efforts would fail to find the right form. The right form of the transparence being sought is not the permeability of an ordained form, but a *formula* of 'dying and becoming', in which human beings keep sacrificing to the life growing up all that has already come to be. To mature in and to this formula as to a way of conscious existence and personal freedom is the meaning of the Way.

The initiatory Way and mysticism

The Way, whose meaning is the true Self, the human individual transformed to manifest the Being in existence, is the 'initiatory Way', i.e. the Way that opens the door to the Mystery – the Mystery which is indeed the LIFE and BEING hidden in everything that lives. It is that which to share in constitutes the Essence of all things. It is the all-overriding Whole in its presence in the 'part', a presence that gives the part its life and its meaning. The individual way in which the overriding whole is present, speaks and calls in a living creature constitutes its 'Essence', the secret centre about which everything revolves, from which everything comes forth and whose manifestation in the last analysis is what matters. In contact with the Being this all-overriding Whole enters the inner being. In experience of the Being it breaks through the enclosure of order in which the personality, in dread of the Being, has sealed itself off and organised itself in accordance with the world and autonomously seeks its own fulfilment. With that something completely new begins. There opens up, as possibility, promise and obligation, the transformation of the whole person into service to the Being. Life then is one which continually revolves about experience of the Being, which keeps refreshing itself anew in contact with the Being and which orients itself towards the necessary One.

This revolving round experience of the Being is something which the initiatory Way has in common with mysticism. As with the mystics, experience of the Being is and remains the light of life and always a gift of grace which humans receive without desert. It cannot be produced. But on the initiatory Way students are engaged nevertheless, continuously, actively and under the guidance of a Master, in consciously shaping and perfecting themselves by virtue of this experience for the deepening of this experience and for transformation in the spirit of this experience. They work at preparing themselves methodically in faithful practice for a new level of human existence, for a higher level, insofar as they raise themselves above the natural level, on which human beings, 'unknowing and inexperienced', although perhaps well-meaning and selfless, yet deaf all the same to their Essence, live and make themselves felt. The new level is reached by people if their union with the Absolute is not something which only flares up in occasional experiences and as a whole then still depends only on faith, but something which rests on a constantly deepening presence of transcendence, which finally permeates the whole person ever more lastingly, consciously perceived and fostered. On the initiatory Way people work at a structure which outlasts the moment, i.e. on a whole disposition which makes possible, and guarantees, transparence for transcendence right into the smallest movements of their bodies. Certain though it is that full experience of the Divine will always remain even for them an unexpected gift of grace, such people nevertheless seek and gain on the initiatory Way a knowledge of the human conditions for its possible workings. They become ever more conscious of the resistances which they put in the way of the workings of grace and they work at a permanent disposition adopted in exercitation and to be consolidated there, which is in keeping with this gift of grace in that it maintains them in their movement of transformation, which then as such already testifies to their having become one with the Great Life.

The meaning of the Way

The transparence to be gained along the Way is not the same as the original, pre-personal transparence in which the Great Life still shines forth without obstruction, as in a child. Something of this original transparence is among the vibrations at every level of consciousness. It manifests itself in the 'Yes' to life that underlies all experience and accompanies it unconsciously at all times. Appearing in this Yes in the conscious human creature is the *élan vital* that unconsciously moves all living things. Present in the Yes is the supramundane Life, as nourishing, sustaining and promising force, as ground-note of the whole disposition. When, however, people are so hardened in the independence of their existence-form that this ground-note is no longer among the vibrations, the Being ceases to 'animate' them from the Ground to further growth. These are the people who as it were just vegetate soullessly. When, through frustrations and disappointments with life, the Yes has unconsciously turned into a No, the wind goes out of people and the ground rocks beneath their feet. They fall into depressions and states of fear, a sort of dizzy fear, as though they were falling into a void that was sucking them in, or a suffocating fear, as though they wanted to explode and yet cannot. Or they fall without visible cause into states of exhaustion, sadness or nervous confusion. But it is precisely against the background of such moments that they can then suddenly realise that the negative character of the ground-quality of their experience is connected with their separation from the Essence. And in the specific depth-quality of their suffering at separation from the supramundane Life they can, if they have the faculty for it, suddenly sense this very life, *present* sorrowfully *in* its *absence*. And from just such a state of anguished No, through the quality of the numinous clinging to the No, many a person has arrived again, or rather consciously for the first time, deeply stirred, at a Yes.

In unbroken people it is there unconsciously, completely as a matter of course. Broken people have the chance, in this Yes, if it comes once more into their inner being and as a factor contributes to a renewed consciousness, to feel that creatively-working fullness of the Being pervading their lives and driving them on. But even people who have been sustained by a Yes to life on the natural plane, and who awaken to the Essence, experience a fundamental mutation in the basic Yes. In place of the natural and unquestionable affirmation of life comes a force that inspires them in quite a different way, but which also endangers them to the highest degree. It is as though it constantly carries them within a hair's breadth of precipices and over gorges and peaks, with the constant danger of being either sucked down again into the valleys of the natural world or of being drawn up into a spirituality remote from the earth, in which such people, whisked off the earth, also miss the way to heaven. The Yes that announces itself in contact with the Being and gains strength ever more clearly along the Way makes a reality in the end of the presence of the Great 'I am', whose spark, when it begins to kindle in people, puts the landscape of life in an entirely different light.

The Way is the method by which human beings make the spark of infinity dwelling in their finite nature glow again and again, by accepting their suffering from the finite. The kindling of the Infinite requires extinction in the finite, again and again. That is the fire, the consuming fire, in which people continually come to know themselves afresh in the growth-formula of their Essence and from out of this begin again and again to die and to live anew, and towards something new.

But there is no steady growth into the Kingdom of the Great Centre. The Way is not smooth. It begins with a precipitous fall, and numerous are the twists, the walls and pits that have to be overcome. Again and again people fall from the heights of the Wholly Other, in which they had found themselves for a moment, back into the life-form of their natural I or, from the depths of the Mystery, emerge to the surface of the customary world. And each time only a complete about-turn, a reckless leap carries them again into the kingdom of their true Essence. It is a dangerous life of a special kind, a life that also knows no rest, but gains its stillness, with the blessings which that bestows, from the fact that such people cling to nothing, but unresistingly, in passive acceptance and in their own activity, obey the law of change. This requires a different

person from that which the world demands. So the world of the people
destined for the initiatory Way also becomes different. As soon as the
Being begins to unfold in them and to transform them, their world too is
transformed.

People who are consciously on the Way not only find themselves in all
imperfection more and more in a deepened community with the Divine,
but they become more and more marked by the Supramundane and
towards the Supramundane. And that is just where 'the ungodly residue'
comes ever more painfully into their consciousness. Every experience
that lifts the unity of their Essence with the Divine into their inner being
makes them feel the vastness of the distance that still separates them as
whole people, trapped again and again in their world-I, from an
existence-form that is in accordance with the Divine. And so, of
necessity, along the Way they also grow progressively in humility.

Along the Way there is no 'arriving'. That the goal is getting nearer
appears from the fact that it continually moves further away. Until the
realisation dawns that the Way is itself the goal, i.e. a disposition that
ensures moving on, a never-ending, and, in that very respect, eternally
creative-redemptive dying and becoming.

The Way that begins with experience of the Being aims at an ever fresh
breakthrough to the Essence, which enables people to pass over more
and more what has already come to be, to relinquish what has been
gained and let fall the façades with which their world-I maintains, reflects
and supports itself in the roles which it has to play in the world – but also
to take leave even of those commitments in which they had worked to
good effect and already in accordance with the Being. Because they are
changing, people are called along the Way to ever fresh tasks. Because
they become different people, they see henceforth in a different way, and
they see different things. What is long-accustomed appears in a new
light, and contact with the Being, which, when it catches ordinary people
unawares, frightens them and perhaps throws them off course, becomes
more and more for them a constant and reliably flowing spring, which
continually cleanses, nourishes and renews them.

Along the Way one of the primary events of all life becomes apparent again
and again. The undivided fullness of the original unity of the Being falls
into Polar tension within itself, breaks apart, becomes differentiated,
emerges from itself in poles that become independent, and confronts
itself in these, without at first the complete loss of the unity of the
overriding Whole. But the more the sides of the Whole assert their
independence and become something particular, the more the Whole is
threatened with danger, and also its members, which, deprived of their
living root, are tempted to shut themselves up in themselves, to become

autonomous and set up on their own, and to lose their primordial ties with the living Being in the Whole, and thereby the Ground of their existence. To fall more or less victim to this danger is the primordial fate of human beings. It happens as primary separation at the moment of birth of the self-willed I, which on the strength of its rational, i.e. fixing, consciousness, in which human beings shape both themselves and their world by distinguishing things theoretically and 'establishing' them practically, sets itself off from the Whole and on its own. This leads in the end to a breaking-test for the ties with the Being. In people's identification with the 'I am I and will *remain* so, *different* from others and guarding myself *against* them', their oneness with the Being, which in fact they never lose in their Essence, is lost to their consciousness. The urge, the longing and the will to open themselves again in a new consciousness to what they obstruct through the old, but which still remains in the Essence, marks the start of the initiatory Way. The door to this Way is opened when the Being, in which they share permanently in the Essence, irrupts in special experience into their existence-form, grown sorrowful and remote from the Being, and converts the anguish of their suppressed Essence into the promising bliss of its release and its becoming conscious for the first time. It is as though the disintegration of the original and unconscious Whole is the necessary condition, again and again, for the birth of a new life, which, in a completely new consciousness of itself, gains for the first time as its own what it had lost from view in the sight of the now outgrown consciousness.

The original and inalienable entwinement with the Being also carries the danger that when human individuals, who are intended to be independent, discover their primordial home they will not re-emerge from the primordial One. The Being as the Great Mother then holds them fast, or draws them back into itself again and again. Human beings stand for ever in the tension between the urge to freedom in an independent form (Yang) and the pull back (Yin) into the maternally sheltering primordial state. In order truly to become Persons, they must become independent and detach themselves from the primordial Wholeness, which embraces them maternally and calls them back again and again. But in order to remain whole people in all their independence, they must still never quite lose their bond with the nourishing mother-Ground. This is a primordial theme of human growth, which is raised afresh at every stage of human development. The higher the stage the greater is the tension, but also the need to *integrate* maternal 'Ground' and masculine independence, by which the primordial unity is re-established in human beings.

Resistance along the Way

People who are really decided on the initiatory Way and have entered upon it have no inkling of the amount of resistance they will have to overcome if they are to remain true. The further they get the harder the tests become, and innumerable are the ways in which the Adversary tries to prevent people from finding again that Oneness with the creative, redemptive LIFE and from testifying to it in the world, which is the meaning of the inner Way.

The meaning of the Way is the LIFE. Resistance is everything that makes people stand still.

The meaning of the Way is self-realisation from the Essence. Resistance is everything in people that gets in the way of this.

The meaning of the Way is people who have become permeable to the Essence. Resistance is everything that prevents this permeability. One factor above all is the autonomy of the world-I, both in the shape of the primary I and in the shape of the finished personality.

The initiatory Way aims at experience that goes ever deeper and testimony that becomes ever purer in respect of the Wholeness of LIFE in its triune nature, i.e. in its fullness, its lawfulness and unity. Every stage that people go through merely in the course of their natural development is part of the whole of their self-becoming. Even the earliest phases remain in play to the end. What was once a dominant goes on playing its part to the end in the eternally unfinished symphony of life. But each stage, like each string, has its due sound in the developing whole – if it is too loud it disturbs the vibration of the whole, and from all the stages already passed or reached comes a regressive resistance in the shape of old impulses, drives, habits and modes of behaviour, obstinately preserving themselves, which have to be surmounted.

There is above all the resistance of the primary I, so hard to overcome. This includes the animal side of human beings, the overestimation of which is a constant resistance to all spiritualisation; the complete denial of which, however, deprives growth along the Way of the sap of life. The primary I appears above all in the tendency towards the securing of life. Where this unconscious tendency is still rampant it is contrary to the meaning of the Way. Its complete absence, however, makes any advance impossible. Part of the primary I is a still-being-embedded in the primordial collective, the power of the uroboreal, the Great Mother, that still rules over it. This is a resistance along the Way that is often hard to recognise, which usually manifests itself in such natural-seeming longings and desires as that for a dear home, a community, the church, the cloister, a quiet valley, etc. All these are ways, in legitimate-seeming dress, of missing the Way – assuming that someone is destined for *self*-becoming and is set on it. But if such people lose their roots in the maternal Ground completely, they dry up and becomes sterile. To resolve the tension between creative, masculine independence and feminine, relaxing attachment in the right way, afresh ever and again, remains a constant problem along the Way, on the natural plane as on the initiatory one.

Part of the primary I is the will to assert oneself in face of the world, and the urge to satisfy the elementary drives in a pleasurable way. When it is frustrated, people become sterile; when it is overvalued, they cease to mature further.

At puberty people come to know themselves as men or women and discover their individuality in self-encounter in the Essence for the first time. Here for the first time the dimension crops up which only later, in the initiatory leap, becomes fully conscious!

The time of puberty becomes for many a forerunner of the initiatory Way. From their first sense of Oneness with Transcendence, young people now experience the 'world' for the first time as resistance to the supra-world awakening to their human inner-being: the static orders of the adults, the sober rationality, the impersonal conventions, the hostility of society to individuality, the over-valuation of achievement, the denial of feelings – thus, before the rosy dawn of the Kingdom that is not of this world, a grey veil is drawn, the cloud-bank represented by the adult world.

Certain though it is that this reality of the adults is experienced at this time as resistance to the unfolding of the Essence, the hindering of its direct manifestation in the sober world of material achievement and the acceptance of the latter's demands are also part of the coming-to-be of the wakeful Self. So the obstinate persistence of attitudes and impulses that are legitimate in puberty can represent a resistance even along the initiatory Way; for this aims at the unfolding of the whole, albeit in constant touch with the Essence and for service to the divine Being.

The awakening to the realisation that the longing to base life on something 'settled', on recognised values and settled orders, which is so much a matter of course for the world-I even at the stage of a personality proving itself in service to the world; that this longing also contradicts the truth of the LIFE, which is not settled ever or anywhere, is one of the first steps along the Way, so hard to accomplish, to the full maturity of being human. Why? An ethical life and a personality testifying reliably in it are not after all the highest good? The 'awakening' to this realisation, when it really takes place, is no purely theoretical insight. It is an existential awakening, a rousing shock! The world being shaped in value-related orders and the personality proving itself in them are suddenly required to take a back seat behind the transforming reality of the Essence, thrusting against everything that has already come to be and is well ordered! Only if both elements in this realisation, the whole fullness of the *promise* it contains and which justifies it, but also the whole weight of the *obligation* it contains, are perceived, taken seriously and accepted can it become a threshold, whose courageous crossing forms part of the beginning of the Way. But it is precisely from now on that resistances pile up out of the antagonism between the well established habits, demands and enticements of this existence and the demands of the supramundane Being, announcing itself in the initiatory awakening. How to do justice to them, how to reconcile them? So: either – or? No. So: not only – but also? No. What remains? Only integration, in which the world becomes the field of manifestation for the Being and the Being, present in the Essence of one who is awakened, becomes the meaning of life in the world.

Heroic suffering

Great is the suffering of those who, in a hardened form, resist life's impulse to grow, which requires them to change from stage to stage. The more they have already reached the stage of perceiving the will of the Being, but are not yet able to yield to it and obey it, to let go of everything and make room for the surge of the Being seeking its next form in them, the more terrible is the anguish brought upon them by their independent and wilful I. And their sufferings become even worse when they cannot understand the legitimacy of the ever-renewed onslaught of the Being and think they have to offer resistance or endure the pressure heroically, and cannot realise that they are in fact generating it themselves, and cannot sense that it is thus their own attitude, of heroism and even readiness to suffer, that is constantly generating fresh suffering. They cannot grasp that what now threatens them like a dark power, threatens to destroy them from within, is the on-growing LIFE, which thrusts at the form of what has already come to be. What seems dark is the hindered Light. Then, some time, there must be a collapse. Then there is only a courageous letting-go and a trustful letting-in, a complete about-face through the recognition that they were standing in the way of the LIFE, which always needs our consent and co-operation to enable it to emerge in us in the shape it next intends.

Despair in experience of the limit is the door to the great, the final decision. Even in the collapse of their own particular order, in which such people, through their ability and knowledge and also with their ideals and values, had, as they thought, brought themselves and their world permanently 'in form', they still try to cling to the old framework. Indeed, at this very moment the world-I tests once more the forces that have served them all their lives, to the verge of exhaustion. Once more the old I sets up a loud clamour. It labels the crisis of their lives eloquently as a moment of weakness, calls for defiance and appeals to 'honour'. Or it lures with the temptation to give free rein to their lowest drives, and in this testing hour such people feel with dismay the unbroken vitality of impulses which they thought they had long since overcome. Once more, too, the hubris of the wilful and headstrong spirit of such people calls for revolt in the usual ways: Things *must* turn out right! There *must* be a justice! I *must* be able to do it myself! And then, when all this too proves to be hopeless, such people try at least a 'royal retreat', in which they withdraw into themselves of their own 'free will'! With a last radical gesture they now try, by themselves, to cut themselves off in the mental space of their own selves from all the ties that link them to the world, 'which is so bad', and try to maintain themselves, secret kings, proud and alone, against the whole world, on which they now look down from a certain distance. All is in vain. The suffering still knows no end. The hour requires something else!

It requires that such people break through their I-standing radically and without reserve! This uncanny demand can suddenly stare them in the face with terrible clarity. Eventually things go so far that its inevitability dawns in them; such people then attempt one last act of their arbitrary will: they are ready for the breakthrough, but now try to open the door, behind which they sense the Wholly Other, with a push, through their own will-power. Now they themselves long for the New, which promises deliverance, and so, by themselves, they throw themselves with the impetuosity and full force of their will, resolved at least, at the New, on which all their hopes are pinned. So, as though it were now their right, they expect – because they themselves want it to – that it will most obligingly open. But *nothing* is their 'right'. And even this sacrifice, desperate, but still done out of wilfulness, this splendidly deliberate self-giving, fails to lead to the goal – precisely because such people still *want* to do it themselves and still *want* something for themselves. Here, that is to say, everything is in vain which people try to achieve or to wrest by means of the will. The rule of the will breaks down where the realm of the *Essence* begins. Yet in order truly to sense this limit, such people, who have run so far in the wrong direction, must probably first exhaust their impetuosity. Only then will they be ripe and ready to change their tune, to *comply* with Someone Higher. And only then will the time have come. If such people now at last submit themselves, at last forgo their self-will and drop their I-self, they can, with the 'handle of the door in their hand', in exhausted self-abandon, find the door to freedom, which would not yield to their onslaught, opening towards the inside, and now all at once the Light of Life floods in! This then is the moment of the great transformation.

Shaken, such people now find themselves unexpectedly in a completely different dimension, caught up by a power that sustains them, moves them most profoundly anew and shelters them kindly. In the highest bliss, they come to know the indestructible core within them, sense an all-overriding Order and in the moment of supposed total annihilation know themselves to be born anew into a more comprehensive life. The people who then 'awaken' here stand on new ground, in a new order and at a new beginning. Everything around them is new, and they themselves find themselves again as different people, but in these different people they now feel themselves truly to be as never before, 'they-themselves'. They stand for the first time truly and completely in the uniqueness of their Essence and thereby at the same time in the force of the sole Being, in its quality as internal image and in its shelter. This is the Great Experience, which *can* be the gift of a despair endured to the point of true self-sacrifice, the experience of rebirth from the Essence, transformation from the arbitrary I-standing to existence from the Essence. In it people pass through the door to that Life in comparison to which all the vegetating in the orders of consciousness of their former selves was only a preliminary stage and a preparatory school. On the people whom it changes so radically, however, it bestows for a second time the fruit of the tree of knowledge. The first time it was consciousness of their own selves and the power of objective knowledge that they received. By virtue of this ability they reached the highest point of their independence, in which their particular nature, which they possessed as human beings drove them into the blind alley of isolation. To the degree that the power to plan and do for themselves, to know and judge for themselves, led them astray into a high-handedness through which they finally lost their sense of Oneness with the true Being, their way of sustaining their lives became contrary to the Being and finally ripe for destruction. The sudden 'recognition' and great homecoming, which in the breakthrough falls to people's lot as inner enlightenment and about-face, brings them out of the high-handedness of their I-self existence and their separation from the Essence back into the great Unity at a higher level. If such people do not relapse, its influence will now manifest itself in a movement in which, provided they keep advancing, they themselves will testify, creatively and redemptively, in the rhythm of the unfolding of the Essence itself, and in contact with the Ground and the One in accordance with the Being, to the breath of the Great Life.

Resistance as opportunity

The fact that the world-I, which revolves round what is settled, obstructs awareness of the supramundane Life and hinders transparence proves in the end to be life's 'artfulness'. Insofar as the LIFE seeks to become conscious of its own self in human beings it needs the wall against which it thrusts, the counter-form from which it sets itself off, in which and by which it can then become aware of its own self and make it manifest. Without a medium to reflect it the beam never becomes light. Every step in the concrete definition of the I, which is turned towards the world and away from the Being, contains for that reason not merely the danger of progressive defection from the Being but to a growing degree also an opportunity for people to become aware of themselves for once out of their suffering from the alienation. This opportunity exists, of course, only to the extent that people do not then fall into the temptation of approaching the Being, in order to become aware of it, dawning in them and pressing into their inner being, with means that would make it more remote from them. This cannot be done by means of the objective consciousness. And it cannot be done through a heightening or refining, however far this was carried, of those mental aptitudes which usually conceive life in abstract scientific terms and classify it according to value. It cannot be done either with the mind that makes possible delving into books of wisdom, into religions and esoteric writings. Only with a leap into a completely new way of experiencing ourselves and the world as a Reality that at the same time conceals yet also manifests the Being can we open up the new horizons for ourselves. What is objectively inconceivable cannot be grasped with an objective mode of perception, however highly refined! What lies beyond the limits of our usual consciousness cannot be tackled with means that are at home on this side of the limit. The world of notes, of sounds from the Being must be heard with other ears and answered with other sounds than those that are familiar to us. But sensing the inappropriateness of the world-related ways of listening and responding can itself help to develop a sense for finding modes of perception more in accord with the Being. It can suddenly dawn with a shock on doctors, for instance, who perceive things medically, that their objectively fixing, questioning, probing look, which turns patients into objects, not only avoids the Person in those who are before them but actually scares away the suffering subject as Person. And then they may switch perhaps to a quite different attitude, who can never be 'fixed' objectively, which invites and persuades patients to open themselves; and then, in a further step, though this is rare, they may meet and open them in the *Essence*. What they now gain in knowledge concerns a quite different dimension; as such it is not to be grasped conceptually, but, resonating in the same dimension in the doctor, it can trigger off a healing word or a healing gesture, which is a sign that here knowing does not mean extrinsic distance, but intrinsic becoming-One, the transforming effect of which is at the same time redemptive and creative. This assumes a leap into another mode of being human, and a genuine mutation along the Way of self-growth, in reciprocal maturing. The transformation it calls forth is more powerful than that which befalls a person in the transition to puberty. But it is in some way related to it.

Acceptance of the Dark

On the way to their particular existence-form people always silence much that would really like to speak, lock up much that would like to be free, and repress much that would like to live. Until this is brought out into the open, recognised, lived out or assimilated, without regard for the consequences, even at the cost of the prevailing well established order, every living edifice stands on feet of clay. Whenever people begin to sense that transparence is really the intended goal they must search tirelessly for where they themselves, as the ones who have settled down somewhere, stand in its way. They cannot get to it by a kind of mental acrobatics, with a somersault that only imagines it. Again and again they must 'die' as an I, that is, as the self-confident occupier of a position, so that they can become inwardly 'pure' and so that the Essence in a constant movement of change can 'dawn' and the Person become transparent. The resistance of the world-I clinging to its position becomes especially clear in every contact with the Being that lasts for more than a moment. But nothing is harder for people consolidated in their world-I and well placed in their social situation than to hear the voice of the depths threatening them in their position, to listen to it and to obey it.

This is true also of the first experience of the great Light; for it is a highly disturbing experience. In order that it may be fulfilled, transformation is required. The precondition for true transformation, whose mark is permanent transparence, is a submergence in the shadow world, an entering into the dark Ground, just after the Light has for once been seen. Just when the flower of Life seems to be within our grasp, when we can already see the magnificence of its colour and smell its fragrance, and think we can already pluck it, just then we must give up any direct attempt. Once again and once again we must face up to our shadow. For it is only in this way that we can acquire the legitimacy for the decisive transformation that comes only from an encounter also with the metaphysical forces of the depths, in which, because they have been gripped by them, people can recognise and integrate them.

Valid transparence, in which the Being finally breaks forth as the Light that has absorbed into itself all contradictions of light and dark, has as its precondition death in an access of utter darkness. But this is preceded by that experience of the Light in which people have come to know their first liberation from the misery of their I-world. The experience of the Being which for the first time frees people from the prison of their I, and carries them beyond themselves into the Supramundane, tempts them to stay in it, and is after all what first brings experience of a 'Dark One' on to the scene, which is no more reducible psychologically than this Light, freeing people for the first time. Only from an encounter with the Light *and* its Counterpart can that *Light* break forth which, beyond all contradictions, beyond light and dark, awaits us in our deepest being.

Fear of the LIFE

The order of life and structure of consciousness that separate people from the Real can be more or less rigid and impervious. But they can also on occasion become permeable, for a longer or shorter period. Causes for this can be events from outside or thrusts from within, irruptions that knock a hole in the surface of the I's 'apple-pie order'. A minor misfortune, a shock, a brief delight, a lifting of the spirits – and transparence can step in for a moment anywhere. Then something New can break forth from the obstructed depths which perhaps only for a short time upsets people's whole order of life and puts them in a completely new Reality; that is, it would if they knew what it was about. But usually they sense at first only the vastness of an unknown dimension. They do not know what it brings them, are not prepared or not yet ripe for the turning-point. Nor do they grasp what it demands of them; and they are afraid. An automatic defence mechanism sets in and shuts them off again; and the surge of the LIFE, which for a moment carried them upward, pregnant with change, peters out, without bearing fruit, in the old, well established order. That people should for once finally let in the New is, however, what it all depends on.

According to the level of their development, all human beings have a certain degree of freedom to open themselves to the depths beginning to sound in them or to acquiesce in the defence mechanism; to let themselves be reached and committed by the depths calling to them or to set themselves against them. But usually they are afraid of the forces in their unconscious, in fact not only of the force that disturbs them and threatens their present order, their shadow, but of the impetus of the new life gathered up in it. In their shadow they are often more afraid of the breaking forth of unlived life, which, because they have suppressed it, has now become venomous and malevolent, than of giving up old orders; for even more than they fear the destruction of what is threatened by the shadow, people fear the Life, whose suppression is brought about by the shadow. More than by the aggressions gathered up in the forces of their shadow, their whole well established existence-form is called in question by the New, which can only dawn when they have freed themselves from those aggressions. The resistances that crop up in the overcoming and integrating of the shadow thus have a twofold root: concern for the preservation of the prevailing order, i.e. fear of its destruction, and fear of the 'New', which, when the prevailing order is cleared away, will break forth and put itself in its place. For instance, the devout mask drops and the animal appears.

The shadow

Only with reluctance do young people fit themselves into the achievement society, in which they have to play out their adult lives as useful and well adapted members of the organised collective – and in doing so they have to forgo the acknowledgement and appreciation of their individuality and the fulfilment of many longings that rise from the depths of the Essence, bearing witness to it. The position, whether happy or unhappy, which such people then find and consolidate in the structure of their community is the background against which alone it is possible to grasp, in accordance with experience, what the initiatory Way really is; the Way along which people bear witness to the liberating and binding, creative and redemptive presence of the 'Other Dimension', which oversteps the horizon not only of the primary, egocentric I, but also of the personality, which serves I-lessly. Experience of the supramundane Being leads in its consequences beyond all worldly ties. Yet obedience to the call that comes from this experience is resisted, more than by anything else, by the pleasure of being at home in the structure of a community, no less than by its oppressive bondage. Indeed, the more people find the meaning of their life and its happy fulfilment in the very place where they serve I-lessly, and in achieving, serving, loving and fashioning in the world, they know that in the constantly renewed over-coming of their little I they are already committed to a higher Being. What more do they want? Selfless service to the values of the beautiful, the true and the good and the 'forms' in which they are realised, I-less service to fellow humans, community and the world, is indeed the way in which, at this level, in the overtaking and superseding of the limelight-craving, power-hungry, pain-shunning and pleasure-avid I, the other dimension is attested. So here 'this world' becomes for human beings, when they become complete personalities, the field for the free play and development of a whole form of their humanity, in which it already seems possible to fulfil whatever can in fact fall to the lot of being human. To be integrated in a satisfying and value-related way in the orders of this world thus forms the main resistance to the dawning of the other Kingdom, while conversely, and apparently paradoxically, a failure in it, a clash with society, its adversities, disappointments and the breakdowns experienced in it, often helps to open the door to other dimensions.

To be in the safe keeping of the Whole of a community, whose 'is' then naturally defines the 'must' of its members, corresponds to a *primordial need* of human beings as 'social' creatures, dependent on a Thou as on a collective. This primordial need and the impulse that comes from it, and its particular fulfilment, represent a contradiction, and so a resistance, to their destiny to testify from their Essence, i.e. from the core of their individuality and free of all ties, to the Supramundane. Certain though it is, therefore, that to be in the safe keeping, serving and receiving, of the Whole of a collective – from the family to the state – corresponds to one side and one level of becoming human, and is in that usually the highest that can be reached, so certainly does it represent, when it sets itself up as an absolute, a hindrance to the manifestation of the supramundane Essence, possible only in individual testimony; and this by no means only when a society has assumed the anti-human character of the modern consumer and achievement society.

Today in particular, when the hostility of society to the Essence has so obviously reached a peak, it is important to become aware of the resistance to the 'turn to the Essence' that is present even in a humanly worthy collective, simply because its continuance always demands the smooth-functioning co-operation of its members, and so of necessity ignores the individual. The setting aside of their own impulses, imposed here on individuals forms one of the main roots for the genesis of the *shadow*!

Between the I presenting itself to the world in a thousand roles and the individual Essence pressing for manifestation in it stands the *shadow*, getting up to its mischief in the unconscious. This shadow stands in the way not only of the smooth functioning of the world-I but also of the unfolding of the Essence. And so without clearing up the shadow no reliable progress can be made along the inner Way.

By the shadow we mean all of those impulses of life that are part of being a whole person but which are not admitted. The repressed matter, which seeks the light, threatens the usually more or less smooth-drawn surface, i.e. the nice façade shown to the world, and is for that reason felt to be 'dark'.

The shadow consists on the one hand of aspects of a person's inborn character that have remained undeveloped, of his or her primary impulses and natural primary desires that have been repressed already in childhood, for example to be able to behave freely, to be approved, to find understanding, to be loved; and on the other hand, of unadmitted retaliatory reactions to impositions, insults and attacks on the part of a wicked world. The shadow is thus a whole bundle of unadmitted expressions, aggressions and explosions. The shadow also reveals the contradiction between the socially conditioned form of the world-I and the unadmitted Essence-individuality. Part of the shadow is always quite simply the on-pressing Life, as yet unconscious, as yet unadmitted, and so a threat to whatever has already come to be. And for that reason, however paradoxical it may sound, a person's deep shadow is also always his or her own *Essence* pressing for manifestation, which has been repressed by whatever form has already come to be, held fast by the world-I. Put differently, the shadow of the world-I, to the degree that the latter represses the supramundane Being, the immanent Transcendence, in its orders, is this very Transcendence. It is therefore also the indwelling presence within us of the One who said 'My Kingdom is not of this world', who called us *brothers* and bade us follow Him. The one who – also within us – came not to bring peace but a sword, who could cry to a waverer 'Let the dead bury their dead' and who said to his mother 'Woman, what have I to do with thee?'

He is the indwelling shadow within us, as a plain nuisance, the terror of the good citizen, of the Pharisee, also within us. Christ within us – the unadmitted Life, the unadmitted Way, the unadmitted Truth – is, for someone bound up in the world, also and particularly for a 'good' person, the deep shadow pure and simple, because He threatens to destroy the well established order. The 'shadow', however, also contains the great promise as the hindered *Light!* The shadow, understood as the hindered Life, can also be the Light in the shape of what stands in its way. When the wall collapses, the distress at what had been repressed can turn into the happy experience of the Life contained in it. The shadow is not only the force that threatens the prevailing order with destruction, but also the dark side, i.e. that which threatens our current form, of the Light that promises us renewal.

The shadow arises for the most part already in childhood. Children show an original faith in life. 'Original' means here 'before all experience', unconditioned by experience, but at first predetermining and sustaining all experiences – sustaining them from an as yet undisturbed shelter in the Being. If the constitutional or environmental factors in which the children develop are in keeping with the Essence, and if they preserve for them, in the language of their stage of development, i.e. of their current view of themselves and the world, their sense of oneness with the Essence, then the conversion of their trusting basic disposition and primary impulses into adult orders of consciousness will take place without a break. The outcome then is a natural self-confidence and assertiveness, a natural sense of their own value and an unquestioned feeling of belonging to their generation. A permanent faith in the basic order of life is preserved undisturbed, and as if of its own accord the capacity develops for unfeigned contact and devoted love. The precondition for all this, however, is that the objects and persons surrounding the children should not contradict but be in keeping with the primary concerns and individuality of their Essence. The I-growth then succeeds, because the individuals acquire their I-structure undetached from its roots in the Being. From this a general attitude to life is developed in which the young people retain a self-confidence conditioned in the Essence even when they fail or come to grief over tasks or resistances in the world. In spite of the disappointments of life that come their way they keep their faith in the meaning and order of life and, on the strength of their shelter in the Ground despite all occasional isolation, their direct contact with their fellow human beings, the world and God.

But when in childhood the original feelings of trust, faith and shelter are frustrated by the failure of key figures, children are thrown back on themselves. And that means more than just a 'psychological breakdown'; for the bond with the Ground, forming and dissolving in accordance with the Essence, is from then on obstructed! People's deep anchorage, their oneness with their Essence, which is a basic precondition for a successful I, is thereby also cut off. In the I such people may live indeed in the world, but they exist from the Being. If the primary bond with what they are in the Essence is lost, and if such people are now set up only on what they have, can do and know as an I, then their self-confidence from now on is only maintained 'at second hand'. They rely solely on the capacity of their I and the esteem of others. If either is present in too small a measure, no self-confidence is attained at all. And so people develop who, with more or less heroic defiance, with intelligence and determination, with achievement and good conduct, try to compensate in the eyes of the world for what they lack in natural, inherent energy and value. Behind the façade, however, the 'shadow' grows, the dark brother or wolf, the dark sister or witch, the 'alter ego'. This is the personification of the unlived life, whether it be the original impulses of the Essence or the unadmitted reactions to the wrongs or lures of the world. The unlived life ferments as repressed expression or aggression – which, because it is not conscious, strikes back at such people, preys on them as depression and makes them ill.

The shadow gets up to its mischief in the unconscious. It stands between the I with its façade, sure of itself and the world, and the Essence, and it constitutes one of the main hindrances on the way to maturity. To become aware of it, to acknowledge it and to integrate the forces it contains is thus part of the work along the inner Way. It is the stretch of the inner Way that needs the help of psychotherapy, for between the distress of the neurotic and the general distress of the man and woman of our time there are, with regard to their roots and the ways of overcoming them, significant similarities and connections.

In the therapist's consulting-room not only the most extreme but also as it were exemplary cases of the characteristic distress of our time became apparent, namely, despite all possessions, knowledge and ability, not to be allowed to be 'Who' one fundamentally is. The causes of this distress resemble to a great extent those which the therapist finds in the origins in early childhood of neurotic afflictions. Their most frequent causes are the crushing of children's independence and the destruction of their primary trust, which are in themselves discouraging and crippling; the lack of understanding for the individuality of their Essence, which undermines their faith in life; and the withdrawal of love, which throws them back on themselves. These are the factors which then make themselves felt later in anxiety, guilt and contact neuroses. They have their clear parallels in the characteristic conditions of life in our time; for, despite all the talk of individual freedom, the capacity for independent self-development and self-assertion is becoming ever more hemmed in or mollified, attestation of individuality is sacrificed to adaptation to the 'role' of the moment, and attestation of loving fellow-feeling is, quite as a matter of course, submerged in purely material relations. In these circumstances the man and woman of our time, just like children, in face of a world fundamentally adverse to the Essence, develop adaptations which allow them a certain security and freedom from friction and pain even in the prevailing conditions. But, to the degree that these become practised and second nature to them, they obstruct their Essence, like neurotic mechanisms, and its impulses, repressed into the unconscious, generate those forces of the shadow which then make their unholy presence felt, as suppressed aggressions, as depressions and finally even in physical illnesses.

V

Exercitation

The meaning of practice

From experience of the Being to transformation from the Being and to bearing witness to the Being the way lies only through fidelity in practice, which is what is meant by 'exercitation'.

The meaning of all practice along the Way is *transformation*, thanks to which the supramundane Being can come to prevail ever more clearly in people's inner being and worldly existence. What is involved is that permeable disposition in people thanks to which the Being, as fullness, law and unity, in the glow of people's experience, in the radiation of their mere existence and as impulse, meaning and blessing in their doing and letting-be-done, hence in them and through them, can become ever more manifest in the world. Since in their Essence people share in the Being, since, indeed, this sharing constitutes their Essence, that is to say they are themselves the Being in the way of their Essence, such a transformation to bearing witness to the Being means self-realisation! People should become what fundamentally they are, i.e. according to their Essence – a way of the divine Life. They should awake to what they are and remain by their heavenly origin, sons and daughters of God, and become conscious of this in such a way that they dare to be so responsibly and in freedom, and to do this in the way of their earthly origin, giving proof of the Unconditioned in the midst of the conditions of the world.

Since human beings, as creatures conditioned by the world, become conscious of themselves and the world in a way that cuts them off from their original entwinement in the Being, and since they develop a view of reality whose limits and structure prevent awareness of the Being, a contradiction arises between the demand of their world-I, alienating itself from the Being, and that of their Essence, in which the Being is present unwaveringly within them. This contradiction gives birth to specifically human suffering, with the chance that one day the Essence will announce itself in face of the world-I and enter people's inner self as experience of the Being, whether gradually or with a sudden breakthrough, and the door to the Being that had been hidden will open. To keep it open, so that the Being as the force radically transforming I-centred people and their world can take effect and keep working, is then the task imposed upon such people. Already in experience of the Being, according to its depths, some change in the people has probably taken place. They are never quite the same again. But even several experiences of enlightenment, in which the Being flashes forth for a moment in the darkness of their worldly existence, do not bring permanent transformation. For that, what is required is faithful practice. It is the vital element of the life now beginning, moved by a new meaning.

In order that the new meaning may be fulfilled, three conditions must be present: the *living* of life, *insight*, and *practice*. These three factors belong together and work together constantly along the Way. When insight into the meaning of the Experience is widened, the living of life is at once deepened, and both together drive on to the next step in transformation with the help of practice, which gains in precision and effectiveness the more firmly it is anchored in the fidelity of the practising person.

A new consciousness

The transformation of human beings demanded by the initiatory Way concerns the whole person, i.e. the person as *mind*, as *soul* and as *body*.

'Mind, 'soul', 'body' are terms that have endless different echoes. In exercitation, by which is meant practice for transformation, *body* does not mean the physical body that one *has*, but the body that one *is*.

Soul means the disposition of the *feelings*, hence the way people feel, the *mood* of the whole. It fluctuates between clear and dark, narrow and wide, cold and warm, whereby both the character of the mood and the reasons for the fluctuations clearly show whether, and to what extent, people are living by their heavenly or only by their earthly origin.

With regard to the *mind*, the field of transformation to be observed concerns above all human beings as bearers of a consciousness. By that is meant not only the contents of the consciousness and their ordering, but also the form of the consciousness. When the natural man and woman reach the initiatory stage, not only are new contents added but the whole of the contents receive a new meaning. The weight and validity of the orders that sustain their conscious life in the world are changed through the emergence of a new centre of meaning. And in the place, or at least by the side, of the objective form of consciousness comes the intrinsic consciousness. When the divine Being – not merely from faith, but from a knowledge founded on experience and tempered by experience – becomes the meaningful and directive centre, earthly orders keep their validity only to the degree that they serve the manifestation of the Being in the wholeness of the person!

When the Being enters the inner self, full of promise and at the same time demanding, the practice that obeys it concerns above all a change in the forms of consciousness. Practice that aims at transformation must develop above all the instrinsic consciousness.

Human beings have two kinds of consciousness: the non-objective, sensing consciousness, characterised by joy and sorrow, which perceives life in qualities; and the objectively fixing consciousness, which holds on to transient life. In the latter what has been lived is reflected from an I-standing as a 'standing-opposite', an object, which is made conscious and held on to as a 'something'. This is the objective consciousness, which aims at an objective reality of facts, i.e. a reality that exists independently of the experiencing subject. The other is the intrinsic consciousness, in which life enters the inner being, and can also live on, as something sensed. In the objective consciousness life is comprehended by classifying it in a context of something known, and what appears as 'real' is whatever can be fitted into an already given structure of concepts (Descartes). The predominance of this consciousness is one of the main resistances along the initiatory Way, which revolves round the 'uncomprehended' and incomprehensible LIFE, to which the only appropriate consciousness is one that preserves the content of an experience and allows it to take effect without objectifying it. The breaking down of the predominance of the objective consciousness thus forms one of the basic themes of all practice along the initiatory Way. Every exercise along the Way necessarily goes hand in hand with an exercise of the intrinsic consciousness.

As the reality of the supramundane Life that governs the initiatory Way, as promise, experience and mission, begins to govern the horizon of human beings, so the necessity arises for a new way of 'knowing' that has little in common with 'science' in the old sense. To natural science and the arts a third must therefore be added, the science of humankind. Knowing in token of our heavenly origin means something different from knowing in token of our earthly origin. Knowledge in *natural science* begins with the establishing of facts and ends in their explanation, the validity of which is based on general agreement. Knowledge in the *arts* begins with forms of perception that refer to a context of meaning and ends in an understanding that presupposes a sense for what is to be understood.

In the coming science of humankind, the depth of possible knowledge will depend on the maturity of the knower, which means that with the depth of the knowledge the number of those who still have any understanding of what it is about becomes ever smaller. Words, images, concepts in this science are ciphers and signatures. Understanding of them will rest not on a rational but on an initiatory knowledge, which is founded on experiences of the Being and transformation from the Being. This means that with experience of the heavenly origin of humankind and acknowledgement of the mission given to us by it for the world of our earthly origin, the curtain goes up for us, i.e. for each person concerned, on a completely new view of reality and the task of doing justice to it in a new form of knowledge. This knowledge, however, does not rest on objective-factual distance, but on the vibration-fabric of non-objective-personal Oneness, i.e. on *love*.

With the new view, the world given, and given over to human beings objectively in their world-I does not cease to be objectively there, but in its objectivity, as its actual core, something supra-objective may be seen. People can be susceptible to this and react to it in an existential way (many talk about it today) only if they are able to perceive it and take it seriously in themselves. 'If the eyes were not sun-like, it could never glimpse the sun.' This dawning of the inner meaning is the point round which all valid exercises must revolve which aim at personal transformation. The new consciousness opening and to be developed here also offers for the first time an existential approach to higher worlds. However hard people may try to raise or stretch themselves to higher dimensions with their natural consciousness, it will be in vain; for everything after all will still be trapped within the limits and orders of their old horizon and the structures and categories of their old way of looking, in the categories, for instance, of space and time, identity and causality. If, however, people acquire the consciousness that accords with their Essence, even the smallest of the known things of the world will seem new to them, and within the shell of the long-known the mystery of the eternally Unknown will unfold. The eye of the Essence spies out in any encounter, especially in another human being, the Essence in the other. In the inner being of the Essence even the objectively present world becomes transparent, and the transcendent, all-at-one Essence that was veiled in it becomes manifest, and from now on will encounter itself in the experiencing person.

So long as what is sought or believed in as transcendence is aimed at only with the natural consciousness, and is sought as a 'something', it will always show itself only in aspects that reflect the character and the orders of the consciousness that separates us from it. The effect of this is disastrous when the conception of objective reality that is valid for the world-I is carried over to the conception of transcendence, which is now also thought of as an objective something-reality. This then becomes a thing, whose reality is envisaged not only as independent, but as inaccessible to all human experience, and with that all experience of transcendence is bound to become suspect as mere subjectivity.

It becomes especially disastrous when transcendence is actually experienced as a Thou-reality, but fear of subjectivity pushes away the Thou, to a distance that negates the oneness with him or her inherent in every true Thou, into a something-opposite that is in the last analysis inaccessible.

Practice and grace

One basic theme runs constantly through the religious life of mankind: the question of the relationship between practice and grace. When the workings of human beings themselves, what it is possible for them to do by the strength of their will and their abilities, are contrasted with the workings of grace, as a gift flowing to them from 'somewhere quite different', it reflects a certain idea of the relationship of mankind to transcendence and with that a certain idea of mankind in general. Thus every religion, every theology, presupposes a certain anthropology, the particular character and limits of which, it is true, are often insufficiently recognised. It is about time for the anthropology underlying our own religious life, and especially our religious upbringing and guidance, to break through the boundaries timidly respected up to now and admit in addition a view that would adjust the boundary-line drawn hitherto between mankind and transcendence.

Underlying the concept of grace up to now there has been as a rule an idea of mankind that has been confined to the 'natural' man and woman, whose self-confidence and whose view of the reality to be taken seriously has rested solely on their identification with their world-I, which from its I-standing always fixes the other, i.e. everything experienced, as a 'standing-opposite', as an 'ob-ject', and in which the world, insofar as it has reality, is conceived as one which presents itself objectively. Without an object the I is quite non-existent. So when this structure and no other is ascribed to human consciousness, everything that has even the possibility of reality can only be thought of as something 'opposite'. Everything else is of necessity merely 'subjective'. Here, then, quite obviously the workings of grace can be seen solely under the aspect of a 'distant' relationship between God and mankind.

When human beings see everything from the standpoint of their world-I, they naturally attribute any meeting with an experience felt as grace to a divine origin, which lies outside everything human and which bestows a gift on them in a way that has nothing to do with personal merit, their own efforts or personal development. No work, not even any work of practice, can then have anything to do with the gift of grace.

Today, however, with the taking seriously of experiences of the Being, the time has come to acknowledge as the centre of the living, suffering, seeking, loving, in short, the real man and woman themselves, an 'Unconditioned, Suprahuman, Supramundane' element that oversteps the I's comprehension and the horizon of its world-view.

When people have experienced the irruption of the supramundane Reality, have sensed the overstepping Something in their nature as the way of an unconditioned Being dwelling within their own self, indeed, have experienced and recognised their own Essence beyond all doubt as their own living principle, their centre, then for them the term 'grace' is filled with a new meaning, and new aspects open up on questions of the relationship between practice and grace. Grace now no longer seems only to be a gift coming to people from outside; instead, people experience themselves, i.e. the *Essence* peculiar to them, hidden in the eyes of their world-I, *as the grace inborn in them*: that they are what they are in the Essence, that they have the ability to perceive their own self as core, promise and mission, *that*, measured against all that they have to trouble about in their world-I, is the gift of grace! To become fully aware of this gift of grace, to open themselves to it and to transform themselves in accordance with it and for service to the divine Being present within them, is then a task in keeping with their destiny. To fulfil it is the work of practice.

The grace that for the natural man and woman is a gift that falls to them from God-without is for initiatory people a God-within given to them, and given over to them to become conscious, the Essence-within of their own self, as of all world-reality, also given to them objectively. Whereas with the natural man and woman the work of practice is confined to a physical or psychical, or even moral performance, which is based on the wishing and willing of their albeit well-meaning world-I, and for that reason never attains to the divine grace, the work of practice for initiatory people aims at becoming aware of and in conformity with the grace inborn in them in the shape of their Essence. In conformity means being able to comply with its will to become manifest, hence being able to be transparent to it, so that people can perceive it and it can become manifest in them and through them in their world.

Whereas the view of the natural man and woman's consciousness, because of its tendency to the settled and the enduring (the static, contradicts the dynamic life, which aims at endless change, for initiatory people, in their intrinsic vision, it is precisely the drive to become, to redeem and to transform from the Essence, and in service to the Essence, that becomes the principle of their acting and knowing, in which knower and known encounter and discover each other in the Essence, i.e. in Christ. For initiatory people there is in the relationship between work and grace no longer a contrast between what one receives as a gift and what one does, but between what one is oneself unconsciously and according to the Essence and what can become, with increasing awareness through special practice, the principle of one's life and truly personal self-realisation.

Repetition

The first requirement of all practice is that one has really understood and absorbed what true practice means as exercitation: not practice for a skill in the service of a performance required by the world, but exercitation for new being in the service of the inner Way. Practice for a skill is finished when one can do what has been practised. Practice on the inner Way only begins when one can do what has been practised and consists of an endless repetition of what has been learnt. When the technique of a performance has been fully mastered, the course of each repetition of what has been learnt will reflect the attitude of the person practising. Every mistake in execution will indicate a wrong attitude in that person. If this is recognised as such, all further efforts towards a pure execution will become work by the person on his or her own self. In just the same way, the basic exercises in right attitude and right breathing only become an exercitation that furthers the Way when they have been technically mastered. In their endless repetition, i.e. lasting throughout the day, in accordance with the Essence, the inner man and woman grows. In this way even everyday life becomes practice.

'Repetition' has a hard time asserting itself as an integral part of spiritual exercise in an age which, as a reaction against ever more intrusive manipulation by a technically organised society, seeks spontaneity: creative knowing, loving, fashioning, acting – here and now, on the spur of the moment! Repetition as a means of religious development also has a hard time finding recognition, however, in face of an approach for which the essential element, in the religious sense, is rooted in the uniqueness of the moment of personal turning to God and in the unpredictability of His workings in man. Yet repetition, as the training of certain attitudes, is the very thing that can help to create conditions favourable both to spontaneity from the depths and to openness for the always unique irruption of the Divine. And there is a third point that today stands in the way of readiness for repetition: the fact that all practice requires discipline. This is something that gets a negative reaction from a generation that feels anti-authoritarian to the point of hostility to any order and any form. For repetition as the principle of practice means, of course, *having* to do something again and again, irrespective of one's readiness or the mood of the moment. Here, however, a distinction must be made between autonomous discipline, which springs from a free decision, in which people obey the authority of their own Essence, and heteronomous discipline, which arises from obedience to an external authority.

The meaning of practice, transparence, is served by aiming in the first place at making an activity automatic, or by the elimination that becomes possible through this of the I that fixes objectively, which always *does* over again what has already been learnt and is worried that it might not succeed. These three factors, establishing and holding fast objectively, doing wilfully and the fear of failure, stand in the way of the perception and effectiveness of the Reality that can never be 'done' and is only effective when human individuals, with their willing, their knowing and their own effective powers, step back.

At the beginning of all religious cults one finds dancing and singing in the shape of an endless repetition of rhythmic movements and the same sequence of notes. Such exercises suspend the natural man and woman's independent form of existence and consciousness, which maintains itself in 'positions', and transport them into the special state of being outside themselves. They come out of their I, in which they had set themselves up, and set themselves off from others, on their own as separate individuals, and they land ecstatically in something more comprehensive, in which, let loose and let out in a happy way, they feel liberated and at the same time in safe keeping. It carries them as in a delirium beyond the narrow confines of their usual horizon and gives them not only contact with another dimension but the experience of dwelling at heart in a more comprehensive Reality, to which they have now come home. Is such an experience only primitive? And accessible only to primitive people? Certainly not. But what maintains highly developed people in their state of supposed independence is something that separates them from the primordial Unity, to which, because they have of course in their Essence an inalienable share in it, they are nevertheless always drawn. And the more estranged they become from their primordial home, the more powerfully they are swept up by a vortex in which they can for once 'let themselves go' into a primordial 'something'. We must understand many phenomena of our time in this way, as acts of release for repressed aspects that are part of the elementary person; when they not only have to be disciplined in the name of due proportion, but become altogether suspect and denied, they are bound to break out sooner or later with primordial violence.

Finding the way to gestures in accordance with the Essence, their training in 'endless repetition', especially too the approach to dancing as a source and medium of self-discovery, self-release and self-exercise in the body, will have to be more and more a part of all education, and especially of all professions that have to do with human guidance – hence of all teachers, therapists and priests. Important in this respect is a knowledge of the twofold significance of every act and of the significance of the body.

The twofold significance of every act

With its ambition, its aversion to pain, its need for prestige and power, its basic mistrust of Life and its corresponding need for security, the primary I of human beings gets in the way, not only of the fulfilment of their potential achievement in the world and the perfecting of their personality as reliable servers of their community, but especially on the way to transparence, hence on the initiatory Way. To get rid of people's hardening in the postures of their world-I demands a complete change of attitude and with that of all the gestures in which it is expressed and acted out. It is true of work in particular that breathing, bearing and tension are not only fields of expression for the world-I: their character in any particular case is conditioned also by the relationship between world-I and Essence. Their character is always indicative, therefore, of the degree of transparence. Every deformation of the breathing signifies hindered permeability. Bearing, breathing and tension can be practised, therefore, quite consciously as media for inner maturing. This has been as little regarded up to now as the fact that we can use every performance whose technique we have mastered as exercitation to further our development along the initiatory Way. To understand this requires a fundamental insight into the twofold significance of every act.

Every act has its outward significance in what it intends; this concerns what comes out as a result of it. The act shows in this what the performer can do, has and knows. Every act, however, by the *way* in which it is carried out, also fulfils or fails to fulfil an inner significance: this concerns what comes in as a result of it and reveals what a person *is*. *Every* act in the world, through the bearing in which it is carried out, can be conducive to progress along the Way to the true Self. So too every 'movement', if it is understood as a gesture. That it should do so requires a certain attitude, in which commitment and fidelity to the Way is demonstrated in everyday life. There is the healing power of the pure gesture, i.e. one that is in accordance with the Essence.

In all movement, not only in kneeling, in dancing or in sacred steps, i.e. not only in movement connected with religion, the chance is given to use to experience and prove ourselves in our membership of and service to the Reality given with our infinite origin, along the Way to it and from it. This presupposes, however, that we keep ourselves or try to keep ourselves consciously or unconsciously permanently in the 'chance of the numinous', i.e. in contact with the Essence. This effort keeps us, as the body which we are, constantly in a certain 'suspense'. It determines involuntarily the tempo of our movements, maintains its own rhythm, avoids all stopping and faltering, performs even the act of standing as 'breathing' and keeps us – wherever we get to in the world – progressing inwardly in spite of everything.

Formed permeability

'The spirit blows where it will' – but how must we be so that we may feel its breath, allow it in and obey it? Occasionally, perhaps, we may hear the voice of transcendence in any frame of mind. But only if we are in a certain 'form' can we be open permanently to what it demands of us or promises us. We can indeed be touched by it asleep or awake, drunk or sober, in physical slackness or in over-tension, but we can answer to its demand only in the 'right form', i.e. in a frame of mind that is at the same time 'permeable form' and 'formed permeability'. We must be open to the fullness, lawfulness and unity of the Being present in our Essence, not only permeable and receptive but also able to keep and to give. In us, as conscious creatures, Life comes to consciousness of itself in never-resting change: in unbroken breathing, in the endless 'dying and becoming' of a form, in the endless reversals of Yin and Yang.

A form in accordance with the Being can never be the realisation of an image in a shape that represents it conclusively and perfectly. Only a certain mobile shape can correspond to the wakefully lived Life, to the living Essence.

So the 'form' intended for us along the Way can only be a disposition of the whole person that ensures the never-ending movement of change. So the goal is a *formula* of change that has become second nature, a formula that determines the entire conduct of the whole person. The whole person – that means also and in particular the person in his or her *body*!

The art of regarding the body, of knowing and training it as a medium of the inner Way, along which the Essence can become progressively manifest, has quite different requirements from those that must be known for regarding the body as a means of subsisting in the world. In the body, body understood as medium of the Essence, people do not necessarily decrease, for example in ageing. They can, rather, precisely in growing old, stay on the increase, i.e. on the increase in transparence. Indeed, even in dying they can, simply by their way of being 'there', even in the body, become completely permeable and so in the very act of dying satisfy the human destiny: of bearing witness to the Divine in the world.

The body that one is

Our traditional view of the body suffers from the dualistic idea of a soulless physical body opposed by a bodiless soul, to which it is connected in a puzzling way. With regard to the *human being*, as we meet him and her and 'deal' with them every day, love them or fear them, this separation cannot be sustained. Who has ever seen a soulless body running about or a bodiless soul! Is a corpse still a person?

If one asks someone, to whom one speaks, what he or she actually hears, the body or the soul (there is, of course, no third possibility in the traditional view), one might perhaps receive the answer: 'The voice I hear is something physical. But what I hear is something mental or spiritual, so I hear a unity of mind and body, or body and soul.' Such an answer is nonsense, in which it becomes clear that what is directly given is lost to view. The plain answer to the question 'What do you hear?' must after all simply be 'I hear you!' He or she hears me, this certain Someone, who as such is beyond the opposition of body and soul. If we learnt to take this Someone as seriously in the science of humankind as we take him and her in everyday dealings with our fellow men and women, a new chapter would begin in the history of knowledge, and also of human education, therapeutic treatment and spiritual guidance! Today we are about to begin the new chapter. We are starting to take the human being seriously as that Someone, i.e. as the Person encountering us in the flesh, who is beyond the opposition of body and soul or mind and body. But this implies also a turning-point in our view of the body.

It is a strange fact that in the Far East, where 'incarnation', in its view of the world, is the primary evil, the body has played a decisive role as a medium for transcendental transparence, whereas in the Christian West, where the Incarnation, the spirit becoming flesh, occupies a central place, the body has again and again been felt to be and condemned as an adversary, hindrance and disturbance on the way to salvation. At best it has had a purely secular and pragmatic significance. The body as such seems remote from all mental reality. So it is really no wonder that when ancient Eastern exercises for the body such as hatha yoga come to the West, they are taught and practised mainly as a sort of physical jerks. If they are so practised, however, their true, i.e. their initiatory, meaning, 'Yoking to the Absolute', is lost.

With us the body is thought of quite one-sidedly as an instrument with which one must subsist in the world, assert oneself and achieve something. So it is 'exercised', i.e. trained and treated like a bit of apparatus that must be kept in order, strong, flexible and 'well oiled', so as to function efficiently and smoothly. Such 'treatment', however, affects only the physical body that one 'has'. Its functioning, as stars of the sporting world demonstrate often enough, usually has very little to do with inner maturity, let alone the initiatory Way. Something quite different happens if, instead of training the body merely for functional skill and efficiency, one tries to put it in the service of inner change. But then, of course, it is a matter not of the physical body that one has, but of the body that one is. This is a difference that is in itself decisive for all personal therapy, i.e. for therapy that has the human being in mind, not just the physical body. No less important does it become when it is a question of guidance along the inner Way; for, just as the physical health of their material body is not enough even for the natural man and woman's conduct in accordance with the world, so is mastery of 'deportment' not enough for bearing bodily witness to the Unconditioned in the realm of the conditioned. The permeability of the body's form demanded in the name of the Absolute is something different and has more in mind than the bodily form for conduct adapted to a community or an enterprise.

What does it mean: the body that one is? It means the human being, the whole human being as a Person in the way in which he or she not only lives events, but lives 'there', i.e. is there in the flesh. One can become aware of the body not only at an objective distance as the physical body that one *has*, which one can come to know like a thing or make use of like an instrument for wordly, perhaps even measurable achievement. One can also, and should rather, become aware of what one calls the physical body as the body that one *is*. That is the body as a materially tangible shape in which I as a Person exist, am *there*, in the world, perceived in the flesh by my fellow men and women and perceiving others.

Understood thus the body is the whole of the dispositions and comportments in which human beings, as Persons conscious of themselves and experiencing and at the same time acting in the world, feel, express and present themselves, exist or go under in space and time, manage to achieve their true selves or fail.

It is by no means just 'inwardly', but in the body, as the way in which one is visibly and tangibly *there* in the world as a Person, that one is on the right Way or not, is up to a situation or not, is strong or weak, balanced or unstable, open to life or closed, in touch or defensive, adjusted or at odds with the world, clear or obscure, with or without 'radiation', friendly or hostile – and in all this, in harmony with one's Essence or not! In the body, too, one knows whether one is 'there' in the right or the wrong way, whatever the inner or outer demand of the moment may be. One is there in the right way when as a body one is permeable to the Essence, i.e. to the way in which the Life might wish to take shape and manifest itself in our individuality here and now, at this moment. One is there in the wrong way to the degree that as a body now and here one prevents the coming-to-be and self-attesting of the shape that accords with the Essence.

Once people have become aware of the possibility and the task of transforming themselves in accordance with the Being also as a body, a new life will begin, for this task will accompany them in every situation of life.

The body that one is reflects, by saying and gainsaying, our heavenly and earthly origin. Thus there is the way of being there as a body which, with its warm and abundant aura, and also in the glow of its permeable form in accordance with the Essence, bears witness in joyful measure to our heavenly origin. And there is the other way of being there, determined by alternate cramping and slackening, which mirrors our earthly origin, determined by the self-willed I. But only people who draw the law of their lives from the heavenly origin will not try to explain and excuse the alternation of I-centred over-tenseness and unstable slackness as merely the result of adverse circumstances, but will feel it to be a violation, for which they share the blame, of the destiny promised and imposed by the Essence.

Three kinds of body-conscience

One can only make progress along the inner Way via the body if one is able to hear the voice of the third body-conscience, and follow it. The first body-conscience has in mind 'self-preservation'. It refers to health, to functional ability in the world. The second body-conscience is oriented towards beauty, towards harmony and towards the perfection of our outward shape in every act and gesture in the world. The third body-conscience, however, has in mind the great permeability, transparence for the transcendence inherent in us. In this sense a person can be in 'Olympic' form, as fit as a fiddle, capable of almost superhuman achievements, hence in the full vigour of his or her physical body, and beautiful too, and yet be very far from all transparence; and those doomed to death can still be, even in their body, in order to the highest degree, permeable to the other LIFE, coming to them and transforming them in death.

We can damage transparence through something that harms neither our health nor our 'image', for example through eating 'just a little too much' at a meal, or – which for young people especially impedes progress along the inner Way more than is generally supposed – through masturbation. It takes away the glow, i.e. the expression of a life in keeping with the Essence, and therapists who encourage their patients to masturbate, as something quite natural which is condemned only because of old taboos, obviously know nothing of this glow and Essence that appears with it. How far onanism is injurious to health is a question. That it is contrary to the Essence is beyond question. The feelings of guilt that arise from it, insofar as they have moral grounds, can be overdone. Insofar as they are the voice of the Essence, not!

Transparence for transcendence as the meaning of practice seeks the 'healing power of the pure gesture', in which people are unobstructed for the Being in the personal expression of its fullness, lawfulness and unity. But people who are in the right transparence mirror, simply in their way of being 'there', all the triune nature of the Being.

Work on the transparence of the person as body requires a knowledge of many things, not only with regard to what hinders this transparence but also with regard to possible ways of removing given hindrances to permeability in the body. The usual gymnastics have nothing to do with this. Physical exercises hitherto have been oriented wholly towards the concept of the 'healthy body'. Where gymnastics involve beauty and grace this still occurs as a rule in a purely secular sense, though a door can open here to awareness of initiatory possibilities.

In people oriented more or less completely towards the world – towards their achievement in the world and their impression on the world – some sense must first dawn for what it means to be permeable in the body to the divine Being present in our Essence – certainly not just in ceremonial gestures! – and for the bodily preconditions for such permeability.

The decisive precondition is anchorage of the body in the right centre. With this goes the right breathing and the right tone.

People's relation to 'above' and 'below', to the world and to their own selves

People's bodily appearance, from the body that they 'are', always tells us three things:

1 A specific relation to 'above' and 'below': humans cannot fly, nor do they have to crawl. They are neither birds nor worms, but as human beings they move upright, i.e. raised to heaven, on earth.
2 A specific connection with the world: humans stand in a polar relationship to the world, in that they look after themselves on the one hand, and on the other are bound to it and in a living interchange with it.

3 A specific relationship to their own selves: they always stand, in the particular form they have come to assume, in a specific relationship to the Life that is pressing to become manifest, to unfold and become One in their own selves.

The Essence in human beings presses constantly for realisation in a shape in which it can become manifest in the world. When that is possible, people are in their centre. This 'being-in-their-centre' of people is never something purely inward, but also concerns people in their 'being-there' in the world, i.e. in their bodies. Their shape, i.e. the way in which people are there, is therefore 'right' when they are transparent in it for their Essence and for the Being present in their Essence. This transparence is only given and guaranteed, however, in a quite specific relationship of people to 'above' and 'below', to the world and to their own selves. How people are, their 'being-thus', which is conditioned at any time by both their inner and outer circumstances, corresponds to their internal image of the right relationship, but never quite. They are thus always only on the way to the shape given over to them, which is perfect and in the right centre.

1 Whether people are in order with reference to the relation between above and below is apparent first of all in their 'bearing', i.e. in the manner in which they live out the vertical line intended for them as human beings, in contrast to animals. Is this not a symbol of their heavenly origin? If they are 'upright' in the right way, they unite heaven and earth in their bearing. Their being-bound below is no threat to their being erect, and in their being erect there is no denial of their being bound to the earth. They are, rather, in contact with a below which, like the root system of a tree, not only does not contradict their upward movement, but as it were helps to bring it about and secures it. At the same time their striving upward does not have the character of a movement that draws them away from the earth, but of an upward movement that bears witness to the life-giving power of the roots. The 'right' appearance with reference to the relationship between above and below expresses harmoniously and without disguise the fact that human beings are at the same time grounded in the earth and related to heaven, nourished and sustained by the earth and drawn by heaven, that they are bound to the earth and at the same time strive toward heaven.

2 If the living shape is in accordance with the right relationship to the world, to human beings, objects and nature, it means: such people are both closed and open to it, clearly outlined and at the same time in permeable contact, set apart from the world and at the same time bound to it, 'restrained' towards the world and at the same time accessible to it. As shapes alive in the right way they as it were continually breathe the world into themselves and breath themselves out calmly into it.

3 If the living shape manifests the right relationship of people to themselves, they will appear in it as both 'held-in' and 'let-out', as both in a self-preserving form and animated by a living dynamic, and as 'tense' and 'relaxed' in the right proportion.

Thus the right shape appears in the trinity of bearing, breathing and tension.

With regard to the three manifestations of people's right relationship, to heaven and earth, to the world and to themselves, it now becomes apparent in what way and to what extent those who have not yet found their centre, or who have lost it again, infringe the immanent law dwelling in their Essence concerning a shape in accordance with it. Every lapse from what is fundamentally intended appears as a disturbance of the balance between two poles, hence as a preponderance of 'heaven' over 'earth' or of earth over heaven, of the I over the world or the world over the I, of the form over the Life dwelling in it and pressing into it or the Life over the form that serves to bear witness to it.

1 Thus we see people fail to attain the intended relation to heaven and earth when – in standing, sitting and walking – they either stretch in an exaggerated and unbalanced manner upwards or slump downwards in a way that extinguishes all sense of aspiration from 'below' to 'above'. In the latter case, in place of a living sense of being supported by the earth, comes an impression of lifeless inertia or of being pressed down. Being grounded in roots seems like an oppressive burden; having a basis, like sticking to the ground. Such people don't walk, but drag themselves along; they don't sit, but collapse in a heap; they don't stand, but merely avoid falling over.

If the upward tendency gains the upper hand, the person gives the impression of being 'pulled up' in a way that disowns any downward connection. Such people walk, stand or sit with braced-up bodies. In walking they don't plant their feet firmly, but totter, trip or skip. They deny their natural weight. They don't stand up in an organic way but are 'distorted' upwards, with tensed-up shoulders. Thus they give the impression of being, as the case may be, cramped, arrogant or 'high-flown'.

In both cases the centre that joins 'above' and 'below', the right centre of gravity, is missing. If it is present, the forces that point to heaven and those that affirm the earth come together for the harmony of the whole. What is above is supported from below. What is below has a natural striving 'above'. The form grows from below to above, as in a tree, and the crown rests on a plumb-straight trunk, whose roots are wide and deep. Thus the right bearing manifests people's Yes to their wholeness, stretched between heaven and earth, at home in two poles. They don't cling to the earth, but have faith in it. They strive heavenwards, but don't forget their earth.

2 The absence of the right relationship to the world shows itself in conduct in which people either don't admit the world as it comes to them, but shut themselves off against it, or seem to be at its mercy without any hold. If the first is the case, people give the impression of being not just closed but locked up, of not being outlined in a living way, but hardened in feature, stiffened, without animation. They are without contact, like lifeless figures. Their reserve is not the expression of a natural, free distance, but of a cramped, unfriendly state. Altogether they give the impression of being no longer figures pulsing with living breath, but of inanimate forms contracted tight within themselves. They don't breathe in a living rhythm of holding in and letting out, of giving away and holding back, of letting in and giving up again. There is no capacity for gestures of inclination towards the world, of at the same time opening to it or connecting with it.

The opposite picture shows a figure in which all reserve is lacking. The gestures of such people reveal an unstable exposure to the world, which they go into without restraint or which threatens as it were to engulf them. Nothing holds the figure together. The power to stand off and stand against is lacking. The person flows away into the surroundings, indeed, sometimes gives the impression of imminent dissolution. People of this sort move as though they had no bones in their bodies, as though nothing held them within themselves. They are usually also tactless; they lack distance.

Here as before the right centre is missing. The centre of gravity is missing whose presence makes possible not only the right independence but also the right bonds with oneself and with the world. The relation to the world which human beings are really intended to have is realised only in a creatively balanced state of tension between the poles. Self and world must each be able to stand for themselves and yet be related to each other and bound to each other. They must be able to separate so that they can find themselves and become one again, so that in becoming one they may gain themselves afresh. The right relationship, i.e. the right way for people to conduct themselves towards the world, is only present when the gesture that maintains it, of inclination, solidarity and openness, does not mean exposure. So in their relationship to the world people appear 'in their centre' when their disposition permits imperturbably the endless out and in of breathing, in which they give themselves into the world without losing themselves, linger in it without becoming engulfed, withdraw from it without cutting themselves off and stay within themselves without becoming hardened.

3 The right relationship of people to themselves has not been achieved when in the interplay of inner Life and developed form an imbalance becomes apparent, whether as an overwhelming gushing out of the Life pressing forth from within or in the shape of a form that has become too

self-protective and stiff towards this inner Life.

There are people whose appearances always gives the impression that the inner Life is flowing or spilling over, as it were, to such an extent that it threatens to break any form. Such people seem emotional, formless, without inner direction or order. Their gestures are out of proportion and lacking in rhythm, unbounded and uncoordinated.

In the opposite case there is no easy flow of living movement. Expressive gestures are inhibited and hesitant, and at rest the figure seems as though withdrawn into itself. One doesn't sense the core that moves and animates the whole, holds it together organically and shines out of it full of life. The whole is only pulled together for the moment by an act of the will and is in constant danger of suddenly being shattered or of falling apart. In place of the cramped state, dissolution then appears.

To summarise: the indwelling Life may be stronger than the shell, or the shell may suppress the inner Life. The 'inner Life' can mean two different things: the natural energies of the original forces or the unlived life repressed into the unconscious, the shadow. The shell then has the effect of armour, in which the atmosphere is suffocating. In both cases there is no centre which concentrates and at the same unfolds, in which the contradiction between whatever form has come to be and the inner Life is resolved again and again. If the centre is present then a person's appearance strikes us as an unobstructed expression of inner Life, and it always seems animated in a harmonious way. Form and Life are then 'there' not against each other but for each other. The form seems neither artificial nor too slack, neither loose nor rigid, but in such a way that it maintains itself and yet in doing so continually changes; it just seems alive. From moment to moment the inner Life fulfils itself in a form appropriate to it, and conversely the form renews itself in constant change from the Life bodying itself out in it. At every moment the appearance is the expression of a Life that is creatively forming anew and continually redeeming what has come to be. All parts seem to be harmoniously animated and at the same time inspired and charged with living force from an indestructible centre. The whole: relaxed form – formed relaxedness.

Just as failure to achieve the right centre always means a disturbance of the living whole, so, clearly, does the right centre mean nothing else but a disposition in which the whole is maintained in a living way within the state of tension between the poles! Where the centre is lacking a person falls from one extreme into the other. The 'high-flown' person collapses sooner or later; someone who has collapsed is swept upward now and then in exaggerated fashion. In face of the world people without a centre alternate between unfriendly distance and unstable abandon, and those who are at odds with themselves swing between disintegration and cramp.

The physical shape is the expression of a complete human disposition. So its centre of gravity, which marks the personal centre, although it may be possible to localise it at a certain spot in the body, is also always something determined by the whole disposition of the Person, which manifests itself in body *and* soul. The right centre of gravity, which shows itself both in bodily and in mental or spiritual behaviour, is thus the expression of a third factor. And what is this third factor? None other than the *whole* human being, who, as a 'Person in the making', is in a disposition that is at one and the same time in accordance with the Essence and appropriate to the world, which also implies never-ending change.

When we speak of the whole human being we understand by that something different in the natural view from what we do in the initiatory view.

The relation of people to 'above' and 'below', to the world and to themselves shows itself with regard to the natural man and woman, who fulfil themselves in right existence and service in the world, differently from the way it does with regard to initiatory people, whose whole life is determined by their binding relation to immanent transcendence and bears witness in the midst of their finite existence to their infinite origin.

The relation to heaven and earth appears in the upright shape granted to mankind alone. In this appears symbolically the relationship between mind and matter. But it means something different for the natural man and woman from what it does for initiatory people. For the former, 'above' and being upward-directed and sustained means the predominance and victory of the wakeful, rational mind oriented towards values over the 'dark' realm of the drives. With regard to initiatory people, what is upright represents the force spiritualising the earth. It appears as a lightness, vibration and radiation that permeates the body, that bears witness to the supramundane Essence and emanates from it; compared to this the whole body in the realm of the purely natural man and woman fails to overcome a certain heaviness, impermeability and a certain lack of radiation, even when within the limits of their horizon they maintain themselves 'spiritually', feel happy and fulfil themselves. Initiatory people, or more correctly people whenever and insofar as they are there in the initiatory relation, have a fluid, an aura, and convey the presence of a mysterious Third Person, who is by no means already part of the complete personality in the worldly sense. Conversely, it is given to nobody, not even to those who have come to be predominantly on the initiatory Way, to keep themselves permanently in this Presence. When they drop out of it, they at once lose the radiation that is otherwise theirs, which reveals the presence of the Higher, of the 'Above', of Heaven.

In the relationship of people to the world right contact with contemporaries as with objects does not concern the same things for the natural man and woman as it does for initiatory people. For the former, contact satisfies the conditions necessary for a secure existence, for a meaningful life and for shelter in their community; it corresponds therefore to the three preoccupations of the natural world-I. For initiatory people, however, contact means feeling-oneself-at-one in the Essence, whose presence in the last analysis allows one to experience indestructible LIFE, *meaning* and *shelter* independently of security, justice and community in the sense of the world.

The relationship of people to themselves, so long as it is seen only with regard to the natural man and woman, concerns the relation between the I, conscious of itself and the world, and the 'personal unconscious', conditioned by character and life history. For initiatory people, on the other hand, the decisive theme is the relationship of the conscious I to the archetypal background at work in the 'collective unconscious' and between the I conditioned by the world, the predestined body, grown in the conditions of the world, and the Essence, unconditioned, but pressing towards its form amid all the conditions of the world.

Maturity and immaturity in the body

Whenever it is a question of the manifestation of the Being in our existence it is always the triune nature of the Being that is involved. Even in its practical significance the body reflects this triune nature: the fullness as physical strength; the law in a more of less perfect 'entity', in its shapeliness and harmony, at rest as in movement; the unity in its openness to physical contact. This manifestation of the triune nature of the Being also governs all practical training of the physical body. In the body as a medium for transcendence, however, people polarised towards initiation experience the triune nature of the Being as a mysterious fullness of LIFE blowing numinously through them, and as a supramundane force even in the midst of physical weakness and outer emptiness. They experience the lawfulness of the Being as a clear feeling of well-being even in the midst of physical illness, as a strangely harmonious condition in the midst of worldly discords; and the unity of the Being in a feeling, charged with the quality of the numinous, of belonging bodily to a cosmic body, which is in us and around us, in which indeed we ourselves, beyond ourselves, are and breathe, like the wave in the sea. To the degree that we become transparent, we experience ourselves as the body that we are, as sharing even bodily in a Whole that animates us and at the same time overrides us, to give body to which in our individual way is our human destiny!

To acquire permeability in the body that one is as a Person needs long maturing. 'Maturity of the body' in the initiatory sense is something different from maturity in the biological sense. The potential fruit of the latter maturity is a child. The fruit of maturity in the initiatory sense is rebirth from the Essence, which presupposes great permeability.

People who have matured are 'self-possessed in form', for they have 'possessed' their I and are centred in their Essence. In their whole bearing they are not dependent on the friendliness of the world or the recognition of others. They rest in themselves, and even as a body, i.e. in their way of being *there*, they are the expression of their inner freedom, independent of the world. The self-confidence of mature people comes, not from a secure position, but from their being rooted in something Supramundane. Immaturity in the body appears most clearly as over-tenseness alternating with states of slackness. Mature people are neither over-tense nor slack, but, as in their souls so in their bodies, relaxed and in form. They are in form and do not fall out of form. But in all its compactness this form is not shut off, nor in all its openness is it any state of exposure. When people are truly on the Way, they quickly become aware of any slackness or over-tenseness, not just because it is painful or impairs their physical condition – and not just because it prevents them from carrying out their duties properly – but because they see it automatically as indicating an impediment to what they really are and would like to be. They feel themselves blocked for contact with their Essence. And, no less than any over-tenseness, hardening or incrustation, they will feel any slackness as 'wrong' – not just because they don't feel happy in it, and because then no right attitude to the world and work is possible either, but because it denies them the form that is in accordance with the Essence. The evident sign of the success of a spiritual exercise is that 'afterwards' one feels more oneself even in the body, i.e. more 'vigorous', better 'in form' and 'in touch', and all this quite independently of any momentary conditions in the world. A spiritual exercise that did not do this would not have the force that transforms the whole person.

Hara

The body as medium of expression of the Person speaks to us in its *bearing* (which is determined by its centre of gravity), in its *breathing* and in its balance of *tension and relaxation*. All three terms, understood with reference to the Person, do not mean anything physical, but the means by which personal potentialities for right, i.e. in accordance with the

Essence, existence and development, or their hindrance, are expressed.

When the body is understood as a unity of gestures through which a person is there in the world, and at the same time as a medium for personal self-realisation, which in fact is only possible from a transcendent root, its troubles never represent purely physical troubles but reflect a disorder and wrong attitude, contrary to the Essence, of the whole person. Work on the body that is part of the initiatory Way, and even of personal therapy, is something different from medical treatment of the physical body.

Wrong forms of the body, especially states of slackness or overtenseness, indicate *wrong attitudes in the person*. Thus over-tenseness, for instance, signifies ambition and vanity in a self-inflating way, or mistrust and fear in a self-protective gesture; a sudden slackening signifies not just physical exhaustion, but discouragement, for instance, or dwindling self-confidence.

Let us take as an example a cramping of the shoulder muscles. This can never be rightly understood if it is seen merely as physical over-tenseness, which can be met with massage, with relaxing exercises that can be carried out purely technically or, if necessary, with an injection; for it is always brought about in part, is not caused exclusively, by a wrong inner attitude. Viewed in relation to the Person, therefore, the same phenomenon means something different. The tightly drawn-up shoulders indicate a predominance of the little I, with its need for security, and mistrust towards the world and life owing to lack of self-confidence.

It becomes apparent that basically all wrong attitudes and the disturbances they bring about in the body are signs of an I that has caused a person to be driven out of the wholeness of life, and in particular to be deprived of his or her roots in the Essence.

People enclosed in their I have an engrained mistrust of the next moment. They continually find themselves in a certain state of anxiety and readiness for the worst. They cannot let anything come to them calmly, and unconsciously they always think that at a given moment, for example of an examination, they have to 'do' over again what basically they are already well able to do and what would indeed be readily available to them if only at the decisive moment they could simply let it happen. But since from lack of self-confidence they cannot do this when it matters, they fail, because they 'do' it over again.

The personal treatment of this wrong attitude consists of letting such people understand and experience the attitude that expresses and generates assurance and confidence. In place of the upward over-tension there must be an anchoring downward, i.e. in the *pelvic zone*, though again the pelvic zone should not be viewed externally as a part of the body. It must be understood, rather, as the decisive means for translating into reality the way in which one is 'there' in the world as a whole person, in the right or the wrong way, in an open or a constricted way. Understood thus it is a centre whose right training can eventually mean a calm assurance on the strength of being connected – something that can also be experienced – with a more comprehensive force. In this it then fulfils also, beyond its practical value, its initiatory meaning.

Just as human beings cannot be understood as Persons without regard to their transcendent destiny, so is there only one right way, in a *personal* sense, of viewing and exercising the body that one is, and that is by having regard to its significance as medium for the maturing of the whole person to transparence for transcendence. A person is only rightly there when he or she is there also as a body from the Essence and towards the Essence, hence open to the bodily manifestation of his or her Essence.

Exercise of the body for transparence means the demolition of all that stands in its way, and the encouragement of all that makes it possible. Standing in the way of bearing witness to the Essence are all the outward forms of the I, maintaining itself and securing itself in its positions. Signs of this are over-tenseness and its opposite, slackness. Each is equally far removed from the right way of being there in the body. Every persona-attitude, every façade that conceals the real, every false tone of voice, every uncertainty in the eye, artificiality or negligence of bearing can and must be taken consciously as a symptom of inadequate anchorage in the Essence, hence of personal infirmity, and their elimination made part of the exercitation to wholeness.

A person's right bearing is always determined by the 'right centre of gravity'. One of the engrained wrong bearings of so many people is shifting of the centre of gravity too far upwards, as where 'chest out, stomach in' is the rule. Such a wrong bearing is the expression of people who identify fully with their little I and so want above all to keep and secure their position. When this wrong bearing is engrained it blocks the dissolving, renewing and sustaining force from the depths. The opposite form of this bearing, often to be seen alternating with it, is sagging or slumping. Here the internal image of the upright human being, destined for a certain form, goes by the board. Such slackness, when it is not plain physical exhaustion, reveals a lack of feeling and responsibility for the right form, without which the Essence cannot appear. People will find themselves on the way to the right form only when they learn to become aware of their body-centre, their belly, in the right way. For the Western man and woman it is certainly somewhat surprising and strange at first when they learn that in the ordering of the body for transcendence the centre to be realised and maintained first and foremost is the belly, more precisely, the lower abdomen and the pelvis.

The significance of the belly, as it confronts us again and again in

Romanesque and early Gothic representations of human beings, and also in representations of Christ, where he is portrayed as Lord of the World, has long been known in the East, especially in Japan, and emphasised in exercises for maturing, i.e. for integration with transcendence. In the Japanese area we find this in the teaching and practice of '*Hara*'.

Literally, *hara* means 'belly', but in a metaphorical sense it means that whole disposition of human beings in which they become ever freer from the spell of their little I and are able to anchor themselves relaxed and calm, in a reality that enables them to feel the Life from elsewhere, to master the world and to serve without reservation whatever their task in the world may be. They can fight, die, fashion and love without fear.

When people are able to let themselves down into the 'hara' and anchor themselves there, they experience it as a zone of life-forces that are connected to them, with which people are able to see through I-forms that have grown hard, to absorb them, melt them down and transform them into new forms. On the strength of this capacity for transformation and renewal they are also able to take the world differently. Nothing upsets them; nothing shakes them out of their vibrant balance. Their heads keep cool, their whole body is relaxed-tense, and in a rhythm of opening and closing themselves, of giving and refinding themselves, such people breathe the breath of the centre. They can keep calm even in the 'tumult of the world'. In the 'hara' people rest in the source-zone of never-ending change and precisely through that in the root-zone of their personal being and becoming. The *hara-no-hito*, the 'person with a belly', means the mature person, hence someone who has acquired what is necessary for the integration of world-I and Essence. Only those who have been able to let themselves down from the I-zone into the 'hara' zone, into the earth-centre, and anchor themselves there, can come eventually into their personal centre.

The search for and practice of the hara, i.e. of the basic centre that allows us to be at the same time relaxed, supported and 'upright', is the fundamental exercise for all right, i.e. in accordance with the Essence, 'existence in the world'. It is the exercise in which the whole of the belly, pelvis and sacral region becomes the reliable root-zone for the right bearing. The exercise for a relaxed and at the same time firm centre turns all walking, standing and sitting into testimony to an existence in accordance with the Essence. The field for this exercise is really the whole of everyday life; for wherever we may be, if we forget hara in walking, standing or sitting, our personal presence will be in a bad way. Those who consolidate themselves above in their I-zone will remain closed to the Essence; those who go slack downwards will, even when it touches them, lack the form to accommodate it.

There is no activity that requires our purposeful attention and makes demands on our will that is not a threat to our hold on the earth-centre, to our being-there in the hara. Whenever we are 'striving' towards some goal, hence fixing something attentively from the standpoint of the world-I, we easily come out of our centre. All 'work' and all action towards some goal leads us astray, if we are not practised in the hara, into displacing our centre of gravity upwards, i.e. into doing everything with our I. And for that very reason *every* activity is an opportunity for practice in the right bearing. Every moment gives us an opportunity to strengthen and prove the disposition that makes us free from the predominance of the I, averse to pain and in need of security and prestige, and lets us be 'there' from the Essence. And to the degree that we succeed in this all work will also go more easily for us. What we are able to do will be at our bidding, the work will succeed, and in relations with other people we shall be composed, unaffected and free.

If one should ask for the shortest definition of hara, it would run: hara is the whole disposition of human beings as bodies which *eliminates* what stands in their way! In their way where they must prove themselves, both as personalities in the world and as Persons-in-the-making along the initiatory Way; for in the former as in the latter their little I stands in the Way. Hara eliminates the engrained dominance of the little I! They then have at their disposal in the world, at the decisive moment, what they have, can do and know – in the event of sickness, for instance, the healing forces of nature are not obstructed by the I's fear, and on the inner Way people who are able to melt down the engrained tendencies of the I in the hara are free to bear witness to the Being even in the body.

If we speak of the hara as the right 'centre' what is meant by that is nevertheless always only the earth-centre. The centre of a human being is and remains the 'heart'. In this people find themselves – assuming that they have been able to free themselves in the hara from their centring in the I – as children of heaven and earth, i.e. as the fruit of a maturity that is fulfilled in the union of earth (Eros-cosmos) and heaven (Logos).

Just as being centred in the world-I holds people fast in what is conditioned, and only their becoming free from the domination of the I opens the door to the Essence, i.e. to the Unconditioned, so too does composure in the hara open the door to the influx, to awareness, of a universal force, in which human beings share from the Essence, but from which they are as a rule cut off. The Japanese call this force that is made available in the hara *Ki*, the universal force in which we share, which we must learn to let in, unlike will-power, which we 'do'. When we are able to let in the *Ki* force, we are capable without effort of doing all sorts of things which we would not be able to do without it.

The basic exercise

How the right bearing, which has its centre of gravity in the hara, is to be created can be discovered most readily by means of a very simple experiment. People who stand with legs apart in their usual bearing will, if they receive a sudden push in the back, invariably fall forward. If they stand with the hara, they will feel an astonishing stability. They cannot be upset even by a strong push. This has to do with the fact that in this case the people are standing in the right centre of gravity. Those who stand firmly in the hara cannot be lifted up either.

The exercise for the right centre of gravity is best carried out, as experience has shown, in the following steps: the exercisers first take up a standing position, legs apart, sturdy, square and straight, arms hanging down loosely, eyes gazing into the Infinite, in the way they believe they are really meant to be – upright and free and bringers of light.

It is essential that exercisers should start, as well indeed as they can, over and over again from this quite natural basic position, resting firmly within themselves and at the same time related to the world – and not think at once about the belly, the sacral region, etc. Only from their supposedly good general bearing should they approach the parts of the body individually, and then not from outside but from within.

In exercising the body on the inner Way the active sensing of the 'inner body' is always of decisive importance. This requires the training and refinement of a specific inner organ of perception. To do that it is useful to begin with to close one's eyes and feel one's way quietly into oneself 'under the skin'. . . . Then slowly, moving from top to bottom and from bottom to top, sense out all tensions and let go, listening especially to the breathing – how it goes and comes, goes and comes. In this way one slowly begins to take note of one's inner body.

Now, in breathing out, without changing one's bearing, without sagging, one lets oneself slip downwards a little. As one does so breathing out will automatically become longer in comparison with breathing in. One should take one's time over this and repeat the movement; only then comes the first movement leading to the right bearing: *letting go*. At the start of breathing out one lets oneself go in the shoulders. One doesn't let the shoulders go, therefore, still less press them down; one lets *oneself* go in them. This first movement is then followed by the second: a *letting-oneself-down*, i.e. at the end of breathing out one lets oneself down into the pelvis. This letting-go above and letting-down into the pelvis are the two sides of a movement from above to below, which by no means run into each other as a matter of course, however! As an experiment one can draw up one's shoulders and at the same time pull in one's stomach slightly – and then let go above, and discover that in doing so nothing whatever has happened below. Letting oneself down into the pelvis is thus something added. People doing the exercise are often very soon able to let go more or less above, but not yet in a position by a long way to let themselves down into the pelvis trustingly and without caving in at the chest level. Here a certain fear of the 'underground' often appears, and the engrained habit of holding on for security above in the I-zone becomes evident. Naturally the movement out of the shoulder-tension into the supporting pelvis must in the end be one single movement. But the more exercisers feel what is involved in it the more, and the more quickly, they will discover from then on how much, without really thinking about anything, they continually pull in their stomachs and go tense in the shoulders, hold on above and are far from letting themselves down trustingly into the pelvis and letting themselves be supported by it. And from this they can tell how much they are sitting tight above in the I-zone.

Now comes the third of the movements important for the technical side of the hara exercise: the right letting-out of the lower abdomen. In practising it one must let it happen to begin with at the end of breathing out. Here one comes up against an old misunderstanding, which in our time has arisen in some people through yoga breathing: the idea that in breathing-in the belly becomes fuller and that in breathing-out it is drawn in! But one must distinguish first between a natural and an artificial, yoga full-breath; and, second, between the stomach and the lower abdomen. The stomach cavity undoubtedly sinks in with breathing out and comes out somewhat with breathing in, and the flanks, too, expand with breathing in, through the stretching of the diaphragm, and contract with breathing out (assuming that the diaphragm is functioning properly). With a full breath out, however (as singers know who have not been taught differently by a wrong support-technique), the lower abdomen comes out. And in this movement, in which the sacral region also expands, like the lower abdomen, the hara first really acquires its intended 'physical' form, which strengthens the whole trunk. Exercisers begin to feel more and more like a pear or a pyramid, or as though supported by a broad, solid base, or as though firmly anchored in a mighty root-stock, which with every breath sinks its roots more deeply and more broadly into the earth, while the trunk grows out of it ever more powerfully and freely. For this it is necessary, of course, that the belly should not simply fall out. It would also be wrong for exercisers to blow it out or force it out. It is right that they should put *some* force into the relaxed lower abdomen, left free and open. Sensing oneself in this force in the root-zone is what counts for resting calmly and squarely in the lower abdomen, for feeling the power of the loins in the sacral region, in the whole trunk. As a beginner one can further enhance the creation and sensing of this force by pressing the fist slowly and deeply into the belly below the navel and then, with relaxed shoulders and without the least movement in the rest of the body, using the stomach muscles only, make the belly jerk forward again, thus expelling the 'invading fist' with a push. If one then leaves the lower abdomen like that, so that one can now pummel it hard without discomfort, then one is standing *firm* and cannot be thrown. Now it is a question of keeping the right centre of gravity so gained. Yet in this bearing there is still one fault: the stomach cavity is also tense. So, while the lower abdomen stays lightly tensed, one must now let the stomach cavity become soft again. Only then does one feel *there* in the right way, relaxed and forceful as a whole, 'earthed down below' in the right centre of gravity and above quite free. And before long the idea of right earthing becomes clear: upward growth in keeping with the roots. The right bond with the earth proves to be the necessary condition for a legitimate striving towards 'heaven'. 'Thou canst not find Heaven if thou art false to the earth.'

So the mistakes made by beginners in the basic exercise for the hara are as follows: they don't let *themselves* drop in their shoulders, but the shoulders; they don't let themselves go, but press their shoulders down. They only let themselves go in the shoulders, and don't let themselves down into the pelvis. They don't let the lower abdomen slip out easily, but push the belly out. They leave the stomach region tense, instead of letting it fall in.

From *standing* in the hara one goes on to walking in the hara. If one keeps one's centre of gravity in the hara, one's gait retains its natural grace; the legs, moved from the centre, are tireless, and one never gets out of breath.

In *sitting* one automatically sees to it that the knees are lower than the pelvis and that the belly can spread, and one has no need of a back-rest. But even when leaning one can maintain the force in the pelvic zone and stay in the hara.

Tensing – relaxing

Tensing – relaxing, tension and relaxation, are two aspects of every living whole. The man and woman of our time, however, usually swing to and fro between the mutually exclusive states over-tenseness and slackness, i.e. they are possessed by the I, whose anti-Essence aspect declares itself in the two gestures of the Adversary that endanger life: rigidity and dissolution. Even when they speak of relaxing, they are often in fact seeking nothing but unbounded slackness – only to be caught up again before long in another over-tension. What we have to learn and continually practise is a relaxation that does not slacken but on the contrary produces tension in accordance with the Essence and a fresh growth of form.

The meaning of all right relaxing is not a comfortable relief from all tension, but a re-tensioning to the right tension. This relaxing, however, does not mean, any more than the exercise for the earth-centre did, a trick to be understood purely physically; it always means a gesture of the Person. We must learn to relax *ourselves*, not our 'physical' bodies, in the right way. This means more than just a relaxing of the muscles. Letting the shoulders drop and 'letting oneself go in the shoulders' are two fundamentally different things. The former is purely a movement of the body, whose success is purely external and without permanent effect; the latter, however, is a readjustment of the person's whole bearing. All over-tensing is the expression of being trapped within the world-dependent I. So it is a question of our learning to let go of ourselves as the over-tense world-I, and to do so not only when we are distinctly over-tense or frightened, or 'blow up' in anger, or hold on above defensively, but *always*. This is an exercise that concerns people as bodies, which is imposed on them, if they are seeking transparence, not just now and then, but always, and it must naturally form part of any spiritual exercise that aims at transformation. For, whenever it is a matter of getting rid of the little I, one must free oneself from the body-form that points to its dominance, or continually recreates it, and is often enough deeply engrained.

Letting go of the I that holds on fearfully, averse to pain and over-tense, and will be so again and again, leads to a bodily change of the whole person. Wrong tension may first make itself felt, perhaps, only as physical over-tenseness. But we must become aware of it as personal wrong bearing and learn to let ourselves go in our whole bearing. Only then will we gradually become *collected*. The hold provided by tension centred above, in the I-zone, can only be given up, however, without one's going to pieces, if one has learnt to let oneself down and anchor oneself elsewhere, i.e. below, in the pelvic zone, i.e. if one has gained the hara.

Letting oneself go, i.e. getting free of the I-spell, must be felt and practised from the beginning not only in the shoulders, but also in the neck and in the upper part of the spine. It is as though we always carry there, and on the shoulder-blades, a shield that protects us against some danger that might come from behind. No wonder beginners in particular feel a slight fear and need courage when they start to practise letting go of the upper spine. And to this must be added, no less important, the letting-out of the waist. People who live without a base, who merely hold on above, tie themselves off from the pelvic zone. This often means repressed sexuality – but in any case separation from the cosmic forces, to which the pelvis represents the connection. The opened pelvis, vibrating freely in all its firmness in the hara, is a basic requirement for all health and all spiritual well-being.

On breathing

Just like practice in the right tension, practice in breathing also falls short of its real human meaning if it is regarded solely as a physical exercise for the sake of good health or the raising of efficiency. It is a sad sign if by breathing nothing more is understood than a drawing in and blowing out of air. In breathing we must become aware of the breath of the Great LIFE, which is at work in all that lives and so animates human beings too as whole people, keeps them alive as soul, mind and body.

Breathing is the movement in which human beings open and close themselves, give themselves out and receive themselves back, part with themselves and rediscover themselves, i.e. undergo living change without cease. If the breathing is not in order the whole person is not in order, not just his or her body. Any disturbance of the breathing indicates a disturbed state in the whole person on the Way to his or her self. Bad breathing not only impairs efficiency; it is at the same time the cause and expression of the inability of people to be wholly themselves, because of a faltering in the basic movement of change. Here lies the initiatory significance of breathing and its practice. The blockage that has expressed itself and become engrained in hampered breathing concerns a person's whole development, not just its physical side. But just as the obstruction of the Essence is not only expressed, but progressively hardened, in wrong breathing, so practice in right breathing represents clearing the way to self-realisation.

The most widespread mistakes in breathing are: that people don't breathe out fully and don't breathe from their centre; and that they somewhat over emphasise or hold on to the breath in (i.e. to *themselves* in the breath in) and breathe it too high up, i.e. in the I-zone, so that the 'unconscious' movement of the diaphragm, ensured only in the hara, is replaced by an 'activity' of the chest muscles. Then, instead of natural breathing in accordance with the Essence, there is unnatural I-breathing, which people *do* consciously or unconsciously. Breathing that is in accordance with the Essence, on the other hand, takes place of its own accord. When this wrong breathing has once become established, it stands in the way of growth into a person; for the wrong bearing that is present here not only concerns the physical body, but indicates that the person, without basic trust, is governed by the I, mistrustful and in need of security.

There are a great variety of breathing exercises devised by human beings, and for a great variety of practical purposes. Their soundness is open to dispute. But there is only one indisputable exercise to learn and that is the exercise in which breathing itself, which was not devised by human beings but inborn in them and in accordance with the Essence, is allowed to happen! In this exercise it is simply a question of listening in to the breathing provided by nature, of rediscovering its original form and keeping it, and that means above all allowing what moves us rhythmically of its own accord, without our help, to happen as a quite natural flowing-out and flowing-in, in giving and receiving.

In view of the prevalent wrong form of breathing through an overemphasis of the world-I, in which we involuntarily offer resistance to full breathing-out and then, because the diaphragm doesn't start up of its own accord, draw the breath in, the basic breathing exercise beneficial for most people consists above all in allowing – to begin with even stressing – full breathing-out. Then the right breathing-in comes entirely on its own. Indeed, just as the meaning of right relaxation is right tension, so is the meaning and the fruit of right breathing-out right breathing-in, coming entirely of its own accord. One must not first seek to take in order to be able to give, but give everything away in order to be allowed to receive. So practice in breathing-out should also not be done only in the sense of a physical exercise, but in such a way that we slip *ourselves* trustfully and without reserve into the outflowing breath. Letting the breath flow out completely shows trust in life. Holding the breath is what people do who distrust themselves and life. So, as in the exercise for right bearing and right relaxation, here too, in the exercise for right breathing, it is a question above all of letting go of the I, perpetually holding on and securing its position and its possessions, in a gesture of trust. For it is only in this way that we can come out of our screwed-up reserve and over-tenseness and become open to our Essence and, in becoming one with it again, free to acquire the finite shape that corresponds to our infinite internal image.

Yin - yang

The right centre of gravity, the right tension and the right breathing – together they find their symbolic expression in the ancient Eastern sign of yin and yang. The Far East comprehends in this the highest reality itself, which is sensed, perceived and experienced as the Tao. To and from this Tao are the two poles between which life oscillates, yin and yang. When Western thought today is beginning to accept the living polarity of yin and yang into its conception of what is human, it is by no means just letting in the kernel of Eastern wisdom; it is opening itself to the fertility of a basic principle of all valid contemplation of life whatsoever.

Yin and yang, what does it mean? It means the against-and-with each other of two primordial principles, in whose name all life bodies forth, disembodies itself and embodies itself afresh, in the coming out and going in of its living process of taking shape. Life brings forth an abundance of forms and drives each one into the separateness and perfection of its own form. Each movement into a form (yang), however, has a corresponding counter-movement (yin) back into the All-One, which contradicts all separating and takes each form home again. So each push into the separate has a corresponding pull into the Unity that annuls it. In human beings this movement appears in the play and counter-play of masculine and feminine, of the world of the father and the world of the mother, of heaven and earth, of begetting and conceiving, of creative activity and redemptive inactivity, of the active application of the will and passive acceptance, of clear I-world consciousness and dark unconsciousness, of the world-I, with its joy in fashioning, and the Essence, with its closeness of God. But human life is always both. One without the other is not yin, is not yang. Only in the circle and in the circle of the Whole does the sign have validity and bear what it means as fruit. Every living creature is an embodiment of yin and yang; so too are living human beings. But they are truly alive only in harmony with the great Law – which means in the rhythm of yin and yang.

Breathing pulsates in a truly living way only in the combined action of a breath out that runs into a breath in and a breath in that runs into a breath out. Whenever the movement falters on one side or the other, life is thrown out of gear; when it comes to a standstill, it ceases! Which is indeed why the Adversary of Life can be thought of as the power that destroys life in two different ways: at the climax of a form's development he brings the movement to a standstill and, by constricting what is apparently perfected at that very point and letting it become fixed, he leads to its death through rigidity, or, on the other hand, he denies the 'going-in' movement of the developed form its change-over into the ascending movement to a new form, and this then means the end through dissolution. Thus in place of the 'both-together' of tension towards a form and relaxation into the Unity that annuls it and brings it forth anew, which is part of all that lives, comes the death-bringing antithesis of rigidity (over-tenseness) and dissolution (slackness). The former is the Western danger (also in us); the latter the Eastern (also in us). In both cases the breath of life falters, and that means death. And who in human beings is the Adversary's representative? None other than the I, taking its stand in the middle, which keeps humans on the go between over-tenseness and slackness!

Right breathing is the prerequisite for right living. In it take place, grow and unfold in endless succession the becoming and un-becoming, the going-in and coming-out again, the opening and closing, the taking on of form and the annulment of the form, the emergence and the re-merging of all that lives in the Ground of the Being. This deeper significance of breathing is thus the reason why no spiritual exercise that aims at living transformation is possible in the last analysis without awareness of breathing. Those engaged in a spiritual exercise who fail to see themselves as breathing bodies end in a spirituality that is remote from the body and adverse to change, i.e. rootless. In practising right breathing, on the other hand, they can sense and help themselves in the movement of change.

Times and people differ, and so too does East and West, about which of the two movements bears the emphasis, the 'going in and going home' (yin) or the 'going on and going out' (yang). The peoples of the East are more peoples of the eternal going home, the peoples of the West of the eternal setting off and going out. And in the same way there are also individuals who are more yin and others who are more yang. The world and the Way are given to them, and given over to them, in different ways. Mother-soul as primordial source and homeward pull and father-mind as creative force and law contend and combine in a different way. Yet, certain though it is that the placing of the emphasis involves differences in attitude to life and basic intention and in the experience of promise and mission, human life remains in the end fruitful and whole only if there is also room for the counter-movement. The individuality of each and every creature determines the basic direction of its development to its appointed shape. The tendency to one-sidedness which this entails is, however, the danger connected with all individuality. This applies also to the Christian West, for which the restoration of the primordial Unity of the Being signifies, not a back, and home, to the Great Mother, but the victory of the creative, clear father-mind over matter, which is shaped and transformed by it in mankind into a conscious mirror of the primordial Unity.

Physical training as exercitation

There are basic physical bearings that stand in the way of the manifestation of unity with the Essence and others that promote it.

People become sound and whole only to the degree that the structure of their basic bearings allows them to be permeable, to open themselves, relaxed and calm, to their inner Essence, to give and to move themselves in accordance with it.

To the degree that this permeability is maintained the Being manifests itself in existence as a joyful, liberating force, its quality as internal image as the beauty of the moved form, and its unity as the warm fellowship of human beings with themselves and with others, unconsciously even on the natural plane.

People's bodies contradict their destiny to the degree that – because they are over-tense or slack – they prevent this threefold manifestation of Life.

A training of the body that has in mind the great permeability for the Essence differs fundamentally from a training of the body that is concerned only with 'health and performance', i.e. with 'efficiency'. But this permeability to the Essence is also the best precondition for all the functional powers of the world-I, hence also for the success of any performance. Yet something that, for a training of the body oriented solely or predominantly towards objective performance, is merely the best human precondition – becomes, for a training of the body that has regard for the whole person, open to the Essence, the decisive and directive meaning.

There is the great tradition of the ancient Japanese sporting arts. This ancient Japanese approach has a timeless and universal significance. The truth contained in it would be valid for us too – provided that for us the central meaning of physical exercise, round which everything turns, were not measurable performance but the human being who achieves it.

In the Japanese tradition this principle is also the basis of practice in the technique of the arts and of war, as well as that of artists, as a means of discovering and freeing the Essence. Here, a fully mastered technique, i.e. the skill of those practising purged of their I, puts a deeper force at their disposal, which now becomes conscious in the glow of their experience and does the masterly deed for them. The moments in which this really succeeds are rare, even among great experts, and not fully within their control.

The distinctive feature of ancient Japanese sport lies in the fact that in the relationship between human being and performance the emphasis is placed on the human being and not on the performance. It is not performances that through some measurable dimension give those who achieve them their rank and value, but the individuals who, through their whole disposition, attitude and bearing, confer rank and value on the great performances. Where this view prevails, practice for any performance rightly understood becomes a wonderful opportunity for the cleansing and maturing of the person, i.e. for exercitation!

What does such practice look like, then, whose central meaning from the beginning is not just the performance as such, but through that the true human being?

In practising some performance it is indeed always a matter at first of learning a technique, attentively and with a will, which is the prerequisite of any skill. But even this first training in a 'technique' can help one learn to direct one's attention inwards instead of outwards and to cultivate the right disposition and bearing.

The more one masters a technique by practice, and the more smoothly and without disturbance the performance increases in sureness (hence the less 'technique' or 'skill' is to blame when mistakes still occur), the more the whole automatised course of the action becomes a pure mirror of one's own inner order or disorder. It then becomes ever easier to catch sight of the inner enemy, i.e. the factor *in* ourselves, which makes its disturbing presence felt in failure, in little twitches, deviations and irregularities.

To make the execution of a performance into a mirror of one's inner order is one of the principles of practice that can be applied to any automatised action. Thus typewriting, for those who have mastered it technically, can become a significant source of experiences that provide information about people's own disposition and at the same time the chance for them to put themselves in order. When what has been mastered technically becomes a mirror of the inner bearing, practice of a performance becomes at the same time exercitation along the Way, and it does so to the degree that the cause of all disturbances and blockages of a skill becomes conscious.

Who is the inner enemy? Who is to blame when the impeccable performance does not come about, although the technique has been impeccably mastered? With this we are faced with the fundamental problem that faces all who have mastered an exercise technically and are forced to discover that at the decisive moment they fail. What then are the requirements that must be added to skill in order that a learned performance shall succeed? People say, good nerves. Being 'in condition'. But what does it mean to be 'in form'? What throws the form into disarray and the person off balance? Anyone to whom the answer to this question becomes clear once and for all will also be clear about the pivotal point round which all practice must turn whose central meaning is not objective performance but the maturing of the human being. The answer runs: it is the I, which has its yardstick of values outside and not inside, and which, in order to make sure, 'does' over again what it could simply 'allow' to happen. To realise this is to understand the connection between all performance, even of a physical exercise or a sport, and human maturity.

The main Adversary on the inner, initiatory Way is the egocentric I, oriented solely towards the world, in need of security and dependent on the world for its self-esteem. If it can now be established, on the other hand, that it is also this selfsame I that spoils a good performance, even when the technique has been mastered, it becomes clear that efforts concerning the requirements for a perfect performance, and the thousandfold repetition of the same sequence of movements necessary in training, can be carried out as practice in overcoming the I and hence also as practice for the great permeability! This is true from the moment the technique has been mastered, and the struggle for unblemished perfection then no longer revolves around the improvement of technique, but becomes increasingly a cleansing coming to terms with oneself.

If those who are practising have mastered the technique of the performance they have been set, the sequence of movements, if they would only *allow* their skill to function, would take place entirely of its own accord and unintentionally (with an 'unconscious sureness'). If those practising are now worried about succeeding, however, instead of simply allowing what they know how to do to happen, they will always *do* it over again by themselves. This means that they cannot get out of the state of consciousness which we call the 'objectively fixing' consciousness.

Overcoming the I means, therefore, overcoming not only 1. the 'vain' I, but also 2. the 'fixing' I and 3. the I that 'does' everything. It takes place in favour of a general attitude in which the learned technique is simply allowed to happen, hence in favour of a permissive gesture. But that implies a basic attitude of trust. Trust in what? In one's own skill? That is obviously not enough! In luck? That is a delusion! In one's own I? That obviously fails. So there remains only trust in the personal deep-centre that constitutes the real core of the human personality.

In this basic trust, when the technique of a performanc has been mastered, lies not only the prerequisite for a perfect performance, but also that 'piety' the development of which goes along with maturing. Its vital element is nothing else but an unconditional trust in something that one cannot do, but which one is, in the depths of one's own self, and which one must admit.

This deep dimension, like everything that stands in its way, can only be truly sensed, however, when the worried and well-meaning I lets it have room; and it can only take effect in the long run when a person learns not only to sense it but also to take it seriously.

So there is a common condition for reliable performance and for progress along the Way. The greatest performances come about when the people achieving them have the impression that they themselves no longer have to do them, when they abandon the instrument of a perfected skill, freed from their vain and all-too-busy I, full of trust to that deep force within them, which then achieves the performance for them. In the same sense, what matters throughout our life along the Way to maturity is to make our world-I step back again and again, and that means ceding the field to that higher Reality in whose service in the last analysis it stands. Because of this shared condition for perfect performance and genuine maturity every attesting of a skill can serve the inner Way. This realisation could bring about a revolution in the realm of physical exercise, i.e. of sport. Sporting performance and human maturing, felt hitherto to be opposites, not only can but should be allied to each other. The meaning of sport should be the human being, not the meaning of a human being a football! Such a turning-point, it is true, needs the basic approach that what matters in human life before all is to acquire and prove in maturing the permeability that enables people, in creating, serving and loving in the world, to prove themselves in the service of a Higher Being. For that, the 'inner form' that meets the challenge of performance entirely from the centre, and not from the will-exerting I, must be sensed again and again in every exercise. It will then become increasingly the secret master of all further practice.

The right form is always conditioned by the right centre of gravity, i.e. the hara, the gaining, strengthening and proving of which stands at the beginning and end of all exercise. The right centre of gravity as the condition for perfect performance, represents at the same time, however, a condition for human maturing.

Overcoming diffidence about touching

As people advance along the initiatory Way, i.e. become one with their Essence, contact with the Thou opens up to them. Becoming one with one's own Essence, as the way in which the supramundane Life is present within one, means indeed becoming aware of the Being as supramundane fullness, supramundane meaning and all-pervading *Unity*. Awareness of this Unity that joins us with everything in the Essence appears in the I's mode of experience as contact with the Thou. To feel oneself 'there' in the Essence and from the Essence means that everything and everyone is experienced in a Thou-relationship, not only other human beings but all nature and also objects. In the light of contact with the Being everything and everyone has the glow of nearness, and every encounter with another human being has a depth that frees us from all divisiveness of façades and roles and makes possible truly personal encounter. Indeed, more than that, contact with the Being releases love – not the love whose form of expression is dependence, clinging and not being able to let go again, or an identification that expresses itself in advance as fear of pain for the other, but creative-redemptive love, which calls others to themselves, i.e. to their own individual manifestation of the Essence, and if need be frees them even harshly from their world-I. It is in the light of this relating of Essence to Essence, therefore, that a symptom of our time, so removed from the Essence, must be seen and revised: diffidence about touching.

The more people perceive each other merely as 'objects' the less they look at each other, and the more they avoid physical contact. Naturally, it exists in the shape of the tenderness that accompanies love of any kind. But is there not also, beyond this, physical contact outside a definite love relationship, contact that is based on human fellowship and a meeting with the Essence? This contact not only legitimises a touching of others but suggests it out of truth. And every touching not only means or creates a contact from one to another but joins both to something more comprehensive, can, indeed, bring to consciousness in a salutary way their membership of a greater 'Body'.

Because the nearness to others founded in the Essence does not receive its due expression, including physical expression, we are surrounded by people who are freezing. Everywhere there are hands that search, as though through the bars of a grating, for a hand to take them lovingly or put itself warmly in them. Should that happen for once unexpectedly, the bars are suddenly no longer there, and a frozen heart thaws in a current of life flowing warmly through it. How rare that is! It only happens, of course, when people are quite simply *there*, undisguised, from the Essence and dare to show the truth that they *are*, in sensed oneness with others. This, it is true, requires the courage to ignore the Life-hindering taboos of a convention that forbids touching. Why does it in fact? Perhaps because touching brings down the separating wall that secures the little I and prevents a primitive grasping, which is bound to be feared by those who, because they themselves are not thinking of the other's *Essence*, might be capable of a grasp that lacked distance. What a happy and liberating effect, on the other hand, an unexpectedly warm handshake or a stroking of the head can have, or a placing of the hand on a shoulder, giving someone an arm or laying on a hand, taking or giving both hands, or a quite simple taking-into-one's-arms – all, without wanting anything, as the expression and plain sign of a brotherly 'being-*there*', conveyed by the heart, a sisterly 'being-with', a human fellowship. The most human gesture, feeling oneself at one in love, can thus become a testifying to the presence of the Great Third One, of the Essence that unites us all, and calls it forth.

Worthy of inglorious mention in this connection is a phenomenon that is characteristic of human form: the sort of massage that is customary in our time.

All 'medically' taught massage is concerned only with the physical body, which in its best form is supposed to be 'fit'. This desirable state for functioning in the world cannot, however, by any means be the meaning and goal of any treatment that is concerned with, and supposed to heal, *human beings*. In the latter, it is not physical bodies that are touched and treated more or less competently for functional efficiency, but human beings that are taken in hand. How little that is usually the case appears from the mere fact that only very rarely is anyone taught to co-ordinate the massage stroke with the breathing (for example, when it is a matter of relaxing, with breathing out), as though it were not known that in breathing in people are altogether in a different state of tension from when they are breathing out, and as though it were quite natural to 'work on' people without regard for their rhythm as it appears in their breathing. Physical treatment does not mean massaging physical bodies, but taking human beings in hand in such a way that they can be more themselves, and that means first of all that they get into their (breathing) rhythm. If the initiatory element is added, that means that the people being treated should *experience* their own selves as who they *really* are and that as such they can also unfold in their Essence. They must then *sense* themselves in the dimension in which they overstep themselves as purely world-conditioned and world-related I's and come to experience this overstepping-themselves also in their bodies. The treatment leads, moreover, to the experiencing of numinous qualities, which is always an indication of the dawning of the other dimension.

The right 'handling' of people includes the development of their 'inner' consciousness, their sensing consciousness. Since it is a question on the inner Way of breaking down the predominance of the objective consciousness in favour of the sensing consciousness, the importance that the right treatment, i.e. treatment in accordance with the Essence, could have for those being treated, i.e. for their progress along the Way, becomes evident. This means, in the treatment, above all permeability for the cosmic forces and orders in which we are embedded and in which at bottom we share. There is this opening to cosmic transcendence in the body. In this 'opening' people experience an extraordinary extension of themselves. The medium of this extension, viewed physically, is above all the skin, when it is experienced not as something that separates from the environment but quite consciously as a connecting medium. Connecting with what?

In the answer to this question the two dimensions again become clear: the mundane and the Supramundane. Many people seem to be enclosed in their skin as in a cellophane wrapper. A good hand can open them in such a way that all at once they begin to breathe with the skin and feel refreshed and also in contact with the world. Touching points into a quite different dimension when it takes people out of themselves and enables them to experience a sphere that has a numinous character. This begins with self-experience of the 'ethereal body', i.e. of the subtle physical body.

It is also one of the distressing signs of a humanity that knows nothing of bodily experience of the Essence that it does not recognise the transcendental significance of eroticism. All eroticism, not just sexuality that ends in orgasm, includes a factor, which can be experienced qualitatively, that causes people to die as it were in their little I and that takes them out of themselves. Whether this 'out-of-themselves' leads downwards into a crude animality or upwards into a suprasensual sensuality is then one of the ways in which people differ. All sexual education, however, ought to be oriented towards this light-numinous element, which even in the slightest erotic touch can create a bridge to the other side. It is a well-known fact that in the tradition of all religions practices have been developed, more or less secretly, which have made use of sexuality and eroticism to allow people to establish and experience contact with transcendence via the awakening body.

VI

The cry for a Master

The cry for a Master

Ever more often in our time the cry goes up – especially from the younger generation – for a Master. This cry is opening a new epoch in the history of the Western spirit.

In the cry for a 'Master' a 'New Age' is being announced, which is leaving the 'Modern Age', grown old, behind it. The cry for a Master is a symptom that the era of the 'Enlightenment' is being superseded by a new Enlightenment. In this the man and woman of the West are coming to recognise that the spirituality which has governed them up to now has shut them off from the Reality they were originally intended to have. A new door is opening.

The cry for a Master means a break with the role of hitherto existing educators and teachers, insofar as they claim not only to impart knowledge and skills to people, but also to educate them into right human beings and for a right life; for in their idea of what is 'right' the decisive element is missing: the binding relation to 'transcendence' and the opportunity founded on that of achieving the maturity that completes human existence.

When people are oriented solely towards assertiveness, useful achievement and good conduct, their real humanity remains in the shadows. Today human beings, as they are really meant to be, are pressing toward the Light and longing for acknowledgement and guidance. But who can take over their guidance? Only those who *know* from their own experience about the heavenly origin of human kind and are able to confirm or awaken this knowledge in others and make it the driving force for a new life! They are the guides along the Way that we call initiatory, because it begins with the opening of the door to the Mysterious. This mysterious element is the source dwelling within us, but hidden in the life of the world-I, of a power, a meaning and a love that are not of this world – but are inborn in human beings for them to experience and to attest in this world. The guide along this Way is the *guru*, the *master*. So in our time, to all the hitherto existing 'callings' that take care of people – doctor, teacher, educator, therapist, minister – another must be added: the trustee for the Reality that is given over to human beings, by virtue of their heavenly origin, to know and to develop according to plan. A step in this direction is being taken, it seems, by the therapy of our time.

Psychotherapy and guidance along the Way

In recent times a distinction has been made between 'minor' and 'major' therapy. By minor therapy is meant those forms of therapy in which it is a question of healing the neurotic, of the recovery of those who are mentally sick. This means enabling people to make their way in the world again and prove, themselves as fit for work and able to make contact; and, as necessary condition for this, freeing them from their fear, their feelings of guilt and their lack of contact. This work is done in aid of people who identify in a natural way with their world-I. This therapy has a purely *pragmatic* character. It will always remain the doctor's first concern. To this another theme has lately been added, which crops up when people's suffering – whether physical or mental – has its roots at a depth that reaches, beyond what is still comprehensible psychologically, into the core of their metaphysical being, hence into those depths of the unconscious whose manifestations have a numinous character. When the numinous crops up the supramundane Life is involved. 'Healing' is then only possible if such 'sick' people learn to understand themselves from that point of view and to see their failure in the world as expressing the blocking of a self-realisation in which their own transcendent Essence should come forth. This therapy, which serves the outward testimony of the Essence in the world-I and in this sense the realisation of the true Self, and is not concerned merely with the recovery of a world-I remote from the Essence, has been called major therapy. If it remains true to itself, and does not still see itself in the end as merely another, indirect way to rehabilitation and making-fit for the world, it has an *initiatory* meaning.

It is understandable that 'analysts' who themselves have not reached the necessary 'stage', who know nothing of a 'transcendent core', can know nothing, or don't even want to know anything, about it as a reality and will interpret the manifestations of this core as projections, as illusions and the wishful images of an escapist I. Much mischief is done by this. A sufferer who belongs on the initiatory level and is not understood at that level, who is possibly detained uncomprehendingly at the natural level, is severely harmed by this – just as the person who belongs to this level, but does not develop in accordance with it, becomes sick.

In the therapeutic situation what acquires significance for patients is what therapists take seriously for themselves, both theoretically and existentially. But this is so even outside the therapeutic situation in the narrower sense. Only what we take seriously acquires reality for us, and the more other people come into our sphere of influence, the more what is taken seriously by us acquires reality in them too. What we regard as their core can then begin to work in them like a magnet, which arrays everything towards it, a vortex that draws everything into its eddy, or break open like a hidden fountain that makes everything new. This shows the degree of responsibility that we bear towards those who confide in us.

For those who are called to the initiatory Way it is of decisive importance that they should one day meet someone who is himself, or herself, along that Way and who knows how to listen to and regard from Essence to Essence those who approach him or her. It is rare enough for this to occur in one's own family; ties of blood stand in the way of freedom for the inner Way more often than they promote it. Colleagues at work are bound to a person in a different way. With them it is more the cares of the world that are shared. Only a friendship that is based on a meeting of minds occasionally generates the climate in which the first blooms from the Essence can risk unfolding a little. They can open fully, however, only when someone who is further along the Way perceives them and reflects back and interprets to novitiates what is happening to them, in such a way that they suddenly discover their own self and take it seriously in a new way.

In a civilisation that is regulated to achievement and good conduct, that gives preference to reason before the heart and that rates knowledge higher than wisdom, ability higher than maturity, it is rare to be perceived in the Essence, let alone to find someone who will look after another who is just arriving. The time has come for everyone who knows what it is all about to become conscious of his or her responsibility towards those who 'belong', and to join them as companion or even helper along the Way – each according to the degree of his or her own development.

The transformation that is involved along the initiatory Way does not always begin with clearly defined experiences of the Being, in extreme situations, as it were, or in the clear light of significant moments. Sometimes there are nothing but more or less quickly-passing contacts with the Being. Sometimes only the breath of the numinous in a dream. But in our time cases are multiplying in which people, often very young people too, take note of such moments and ask themselves in wonder what they may be. With awareness of such moments, and with taking them seriously, the Way can begin which points beyond all therapy; but it does not do so of necessity. 'Major' therapy is indeed therapy that is not concerned primarily with people's fitness for the world, in which they function, possibly even at the cost of their Essence, smoothly and painlessly. It is concerned primarily with self-realisation from the Essence. But with that the area of pragmatic therapy has still not necessarily been left behind, so that initiatory transformation has become the decisive *meaning* of the work. This occurs only when it is a question neither of adaptation to the world and the relief of pain, nor merely of a 'self'-realisation in which the yardstick of success is not still in the end fitness for the world, but solely of permeability for the Essence, hence when the 'true self' is conceived as the place in which the Being can experience and manifest itself in the world even in the language of this individuality. The emphasis then lies on the becoming-manifest of the Being and not on the person's conformity to the world. Only when in addition people no longer seek transparence for transcendence for their own sake, but transparence for their Essence for the sake of transcendence, and are resolved, therefore, solely on maturing for service to the Being, is the initiatory level truly reached. A life is 'initiatory' only when it stands unambiguously in service to the 'Great Third Person'. So long as contact with the Being is sought merely for the sake of the restored self, it is still therapy. Only when the self-realising process of the Self is accepted for the sake of the Being at any price, whatever may be the pains or passing loss of fitness for the world that it brings, only then has the Way of initiation been trodden.

A different question is how far the Way of the initiate requires and assumes knowledge of depth-psychology and also of psychotherapeutic work. A settling of the unconscious through depth-psychology is indeed necessary. Without it people easily fall prey to their illusions, which make them believe that transcendence, and hence transparence, is closer than it really is. And when people, in spiritual exercise for instance, keep themselves turned only towards the light, and ignore the dark within themselves, the devil will stay at their backs. When the foundations are rotten, the fine edifice remains in danger.

  Like practice in perceiving the numinous and taking it seriously, the investigation of what separates people, in their consciousness and in the unconscious, from the Reality of the Being appearing in the numinous is part of the work along the initiatory Way. Conversely, a therapy that explores the unconscious cleanly and works through its complexes can do essential preliminary work; indeed, when it takes the Essence seriously, it can become the starting-point and rousing-call for a development that ends in the initiatory sphere.

When, however, it is a question of more than the recovery of a well functioning world-I there must be, in addition to the expert resolution of obdurate complexes and fixed mechanisms, a transcending of the form of consciousness that with its fixing dominates the natural world-I, whether the I is I-like or selfless. Only then, with the overcoming of the predominance of the all-objectifying consciousness, does any guidance along the Way become possible which aims at more than adaptation to the world of people not yet awake to the Essence and the mere recovery of their natural capacity for enjoyment, work and love in the world. Only when the spirit of a healing art is that spiritual Spirit which is born in experience of the Being, which has been formed into the most inwardly lived law and image, and which has become the responsible, controlling consciousness, does that Light dawn, that Light of fellow-human radiation, which has the power to enlighten at the same time as it heals. The work to be done in initiatory guidance on overcoming the dominance of the objective consciousness assumes, however, that one knows one's own limits, and that one is disposed to give credit to a rationally incomprehensible Reality, and hence prepared to take seriously, and to develop, forms of consciousness that can do justice to it.

Just as the reality in which values count is different from that in which facts exist; just as understanding a mental connection means something different from explaining a process; and perceiving a human being as a Person something different from explaining and understanding objects or mental connections; so transcendence summons human beings to quite other responses than facts, mental connections or Persons. What is involved here is an all-transforming, redeeming and binding feeling-at-one and becoming-one in the Essence, which by no means sweeps aside all the explaining, understanding and fellow-human perceiving in the world, but sweeps it into a quite different, Supramundane context, which calls for completely different forms of cognition. And it is out of this that the New Age, a new natural science, a new faculty of arts and a new science of humankind will develop.

All world religions or religious philosophies grow from a sorrowful form of existence, in which human beings having outgrown the paradise of childhood and the primordial, prehistoric condition, suffer from the separation and long to 'find their way home', so that in finding a new wholeness the circle shall again be closed. So right help along the Way means guiding people to their Essence-ground and re-rooting them there and making-conscious and developing the greater Subject within them, in which already in embryo, as possibility and necessity, they always contain their becoming-whole-again after the splitting-up. In this sense the summoning, the causing-to-be-discovered and cultivating of the deep-person, who reflects the Whole, is work in keeping with the Essence on those who are looking for themselves in the Essence.

'Viewed methodologically, existential help along the Way, i.e. help that is initiatory and not conceived purely psychologically and pragmatically, aims from the beginning at awakening the overlaid or as yet unconscious forces of the Essence and giving them encouragement. In anamnesis, therefore, accounts of experiences that "broke through", kindled or made a direct impact on the reality of an existence directed to rational and practical ends are taken especially seriously. The significance of the special numinous quality of such experiences cannot escape anyone who has been brought to take seriously the deep dimension of life and its inherent content of truth. Anyone who is still unsure will have his or her perceptive faculty awakened for events with a transcendent content and will be encouraged also to get consciously involved more and more in comprehending a potential of experience of higher dimensions. What seemed illegitimate or unimportant thus becomes legitimate. What was "mysterious" in the limited view of the old reality receives the status of equality and a rightful place-value in the course of the widening and deepening of consciousness. The supra-real becomes real. The rationally real is joined by a transcendentally real with the promise of opening human beings to a "transcendental realism" (Evola). The irrational is thus "disenchanted", since in the new age of mankind, it is perceived and admitted as natural reality – and finally becomes the actual bread of life.'*

Master – pupil – Way

The New Age, which is determined by taking seriously experience of the Being, also creates through this a new relationship between those who enter it and there unfold. A community of seekers is springing up, who recognise each other as brothers and sisters in the Being, members of one family, who understand each other across the boundaries of space and time. The long-dead speak to one as though they were physically present in the room; old and young meet in timeless nearness. Walls that exist for the natural man and woman, as yet untouched by the Being, through racial differences, an alien intellectual tradition, a different religion or other class distinctions, vanish – and it is as though one found oneself with the others in the train of a vast procession of seekers, who are striding along, across ages and zones, coming from many directions, of different origin and burdened with a different fate, dressed in different garments, each for themselves and yet hand in hand with the others, the same unknown goal in view, driven by the same longing, drawn by the same star. It is as though in this train Life were growing together again into its Wholeness; as though, having been deprived of its Essence-roots, having been dismembered and fallen apart without Essence, it is now on the point of finding itself again in the glow of its fullness, its order and Unity.

In the great train of this Life, discovering itself anew out of the power of the reawakening LIFE, all who compose it discover that they are now

*Maria Hippius, *Transzendenz als Erfahrung.*

on a *Way*, along which, if they have once been touched inalienably by the Being, they are in need of guidance, hence of a guide, of a *Master*, whom they need as *pupils* – in order to become the ones who in a happy hour they recognised themselves for a moment to be.

Just as people cannot mature to their true selves without contact with their deepest core, the Essence, which itself is not conditioned by the world, so, conversely, awareness of the core, as we are seeing today, results in a longing for genuine self-development and guidance along the Way. The distress of unfulfilled Essencehood, once it is known as such, cannot be relieved either through more success in the world or through a return to faith; for it springs indeed from a situation in which people no longer find their fulfilment in worldly achievement and are no longer sustained by their faith. Thus the longing for guidance along the inner *Way* has become imperative. And anyone who longs for a Master has become a pupil.

The Master

The Master is the answer to a question that is posed in a quite definite inner situation, and only at a definite stage of human development. It is when people have got into a blind alley, into an inner distress from which no doctor can help them, which they cannot cope with themselves, and in which their faith is also no help. But they sense something and seek something which is promised and given over to them deep within them and which could at the same time be the real fulfilment of their lives. They sense it on the strength of a special experience. Somehow such people have come into contact with the supramundane Being, with the Divine, in the bliss of proximity or in the distress of its remoteness. It is different from what they had sought hitherto within the framework of their usual life and spiritual background. What actually happened they themselves don't know; they only know that what matters is to get into permanent contact with what touched them at the time. The distress to which they have to respond is not the suffering of a physical or mental disability in respect of the world, but is now the suffering of being separated from the divine Ground of their life, precisely *because* they have experienced it for a moment deep within them! To whom should they go, those who suffer from this suffering? Not to a doctor, who as a doctor knows nothing about it, who would probably say it was not a medical matter, would perhaps prescribe them a sedative or refer them to a psychiatrist. But they are also afraid of psychologists or psycho-therapists, who might well 'explain' their most precious experience as due to something else, or declare it to be an illusion, an inflation or a projection. Nothing is more terrible and hopeless in such a situation than to have entrusted oneself to someone who, because they themselves are unaware of this experience, misinterpret what has occurred in it, for example interpret Essence-experience as a puffing-up of the I. But neither does one want to go to a priest or minister, for fear they might doubt the validity of the experience from their theological standpoint, dismiss it as something purely 'natural' or 'subjective', or even try to bring the seeker of advice and help back to the bosom of the mother church, which, it might be suggested, had just been outgrown. One is looking for someone quite different – one is looking for a Master.

The word 'Master' denotes three different things: the Eternal Master, the Master in the flesh and the inner Master.

The Eternal Master is an imago of life which is seen as a primordial mental picture, an idea, an archetype. The Master in the flesh is the realisation of this idea in historical reality. The inner Master is the awakened potential within a person, as promise, experience and mission, to realise the Eternal Master in bodily shape.

The 'Master' – whether as idea, bodily reality or inner mission – always 'means' the LIFE become human, the supramundane Life endlessly self-generating, become manifest in the world in human shape.

There is a Master only with reference to someone who unconditionally seeks the *Way* to this shape: that is the *pupil*. So there is a Master only in conjunction with the Way and the pupil.

Master–pupil–Way, this is the trinity in token of which the door opens to the Mysterious, i.e. to the Kingdom that is not of this world. It is the medium in which and through which the Infinite can take shape in the finite, the Life beyond space and time in our space-time world against all resistance and under all conditions. To let the Life in its urge to become manifest become conscious, to acknowledge it as the decisive commitment for everything and to follow the 'Way' according to plan – this is only possible for people at the initiatory stage of their development. Only when they have come to know themselves in the Essence as that which was being sought, which is given to them, and given over to them, to become fully conscious and take shape in the world, their urge to self-realisation from the Essence, therefore, bestowed on them as a 'Must-May-Should', only then do they find themselves eager for the Way, in need of a Master, ready as pupils.

The idea which the word 'Master' denotes is that of the *homo maximus*, the universal man, in whom the Being, the Great LIFE in its totality – as fullness, law and Unity – become manifest in human shape, as it makes itself felt in the world, transforming and regenerating, in action that is both superior to the world and of force in the world. In the real Master pupils see the realisation of the idea awakened in their own selves as potential, which they themselves hope and are disposed to realise, along the Way shown by the Master.

Like the Master, the pupil and the Way exist in threefold fashion: as idea, as bodily reality and as inner reality.

The inner Master

Whenever in the working together of Master and pupil the Being has been able to enter existence, the Supramundane become mundane in a human way; whenever pupils have stepped through the door of transformation, on the Way to a disposition in which step by step they can liberate the truth dwelling within them and become more and more witnesses to the LIFE, this has always taken place at two levels: at the level of the external, space-time world, where a Master has appeared, an actual human being encountering another human being, the pupil; and, on the other hand, in the interior of the seekers themselves. There the Master is not a human being who encounters pupils externally, but an authority within them and for them. All of us are this ourselves by virtue of our non-finite origin, are pupil and Master within us, are so out of distress and by virtue of our supramundane Essence, which presses within us to its self-realisation in a worldly shape. And so the inner Master is the prerequisite for the seeking, finding and working of a Master in the flesh in the world.

All who become ripe for the Way and long for a Master, because they need guidance, but who find no one in their vicinity to meet their demand, can know that they have the Master within them as archetype, they themselves as inner Master. If this were not so, they would not be able to find the Master externally either. Even if they were to meet him, they would not recognise him. One is oneself the inner Master as the potential, pressing unconsciously to conscious realisation, *of* the person who one could and should be. To sense the inner Master, i.e. this potential, to recognise it and acknowledge it, presupposes a certain *stage* of development.

To acknowledge the Master within one has nothing to do with arrogance. To accept the burden of the Way that now lies ahead demands real humility. There is also false modesty which in fact is only fear of greater responsibility. It stands in the way of the emergence of the Master.

The sensing and acknowledging of the inner Master as a disposition to 'be like God', to be a citizen of the Kingdom that is not of this world, is the necessary condition for the autonomous power of the Way, superior to all worldly limitation, to become effective. One could not say of a person that he or she had missed the Way if one had not granted that in principle they might have been able to follow it. It is certainly not for everyone – but for everyone who has the maturity for the leap to the stage of the initiate.

The Master in the flesh

The word 'Master', insofar as it is a matter of an historically real figure, means a person in whom the Life is fully present. It has asserted itself in his or her living and understanding, is present as effective force and there in bodily shape. In the Master, the LIFE has become conscious of its own self in lived truth in the human sphere, released for creative freedom, given the capacity for regenerative guiding power and freed for transformation that is no longer to be checked.

Thus the Master in the flesh has reached a supreme form of human existence, a perfect figure of the Way, because he (or she) never gets to himself, never stands still, because he has become a part of the *Way*.

Marked and charged, directed and delegated by the greater Life, the Master is the Being grown ripe to manifest the Supramundane in a human individual. He has overstepped what obstructed the coming forth of the LIFE. He embodies, while remaining at the same time completely human, a suprahuman rank. His thinking and acting are no longer governed by the social, moral or theological demands and orderings of the world, for he stands in the freedom of the Supramundane. The Master may respect the orderings of the world, but he is not subject to them. So he constantly becomes a nuisance. The truth of the LIFE tolerates what has come to be only insofar as it does not disturb the coming-to-be of what has not as yet come to be. The prevailing of the Infinite in the finite shatters every finite form.

The Master does not fulfil any conception of an ideal, 'right' human being. He does not correspond to the image of what one ought to be in the sense of the conventional values of the beautiful, the true and the good. What comes from the Master is an outrage to the worthy citizen, just as the latter is an inexhaustible target for the Master's sharp arrows. The Master is no consolidating element, but a revolutionary figure. One never knows what is coming next. He is as unpredictable and con-tradictory as Life. He brings not peace but a sword.

The Master is Life with its death lying before new Life, dangerous, incomprehensible and hard. Human beings strive for security and harmony; the Master shoos away what has just settled, overturns what was thought to stand fast, looses what was tied; for going is what is meant to be, never standing fast; moving on, not arriving; transformation, not completion. Life exists only in transition. The Master keeps Life in eternal transition.

In the Master the Being becomes manifest in its triune nature. He represents the fullness of the Being, which becomes perceptible in his original force and his power superior to death. He gives effect to the lawfulness of the Being, which is evident in his superior rank. From this he acts as a figure in accordance with the Being, even without 'doing' anything. The Master embodies the Unity of the Being, which can be sensed in his primordial solidarity with all that lives, in the depth of his humanity and in a love that no longer has much to do with a 'feeling'. That marks his 'stage'. Thus the three primordial qualities of the Essence are peculiar to the Master: power, rank and 'stage'.

The pupil

The awakening as pupil is not always grounded in a great event. The most insignificant thing can suddenly cause the inner turning-point; for the awakening as pupil has always been long prepared in the suffering of the Essence from want of air. The greater the distress from the Essence, the greater the chance that something trivial will create the turning-point, something that makes the chord of the Essence begin to sound, and now quite unexpectedly brings to light the Unknown, the Mysterious.

Such people are touched by the great Unknown. For a moment it throws them into confusion; they are delighted and dismayed and, perhaps for a fraction of a second, they refresh themselves at the infinite Source.

Now, however, when such an event does not rush by and evaporate like a mood, but those concerned become aware of it as promise, commitment and mission, and are ready to obey the call, it means their awakening as pupil.

Who, then, may call themselves pupil? Only those who have been seized to their depths by longing, who, driven to the limit by distress, believe all must be up with them if they cannot break through.

Only those who have been gripped by the heart's unease, which will not let them go again until it is stilled.

Only those who know that once they have started upon the Way they cannot go back, and are ready to let themselves be guided and to obey.

Only those who, capable of great trust, can follow when they no longer understand and are ready for every test.

Only those who can be hard on themselves and are ready, for the sake of the One that is pressing within them to the Light, to leave everything.

Only those who, because they have been gripped by the Unconditioned, accept all conditions and bear the rigour of the Way along which the Master is guiding them.

Guidance along the Way also always has its limits, in the one who is guiding as well as in the one who is guided, and the awakening and the breakthrough of the Essence is also always a grace. One cannot 'do' it, but one can 'make' the opportunity for the breakthrough. It *is* blocked when helpers are trapped in ideas and attitudes in which the Essence as basic power and source of Life is not taken seriously, either for themselves or for the other. What is decisive is the drive of the Essence, inducing inner maturity in secret, to find admittance in the human consciousness. In most cases, however, the Essence will only go through doors, even ones that are already open, if it is called. That is how the Master looks at his pupils. In the glow of their eye, in the timbre of their voice, in the flow of their gestures he, or she, senses out the character and position of their Essence on its way to manifestation in the physical self. He is focused on this Essence in advance, and ready to use every means to address it from Essence to Essence and bring it to sound in the other. From this relation of Essence to Essence, in which he is fundamentally at one with his pupil, he draws the wealth of his ever-original ideas and equally the strength for a supra-personal love, whose radiation and severity continually call out the other's Essence anew.

All or *nothing* looms large beyond the threshold across which pupils enter the area of practice. They leave everything behind; only then indeed can they grasp that what confronts them in the Master is not arbitrariness, but perceptive wisdom, which, aimed straight at their Essence, seizes upon every means to bring it to life; for the meaning of dying, continually demanded of them, is not death, but the LIFE that is beyond life and death.

VII

Meditation and the meditative life

The meaning of meditative exercises

Exercises of many different kinds are being done today that appear to have a meditative character – relaxation exercises, exercises in stillness, Hatha-Yoga, transcendental meditation, autogenous training and Za-Zen, amongst others. Under whatever title such exercises may go, one must always ask: For what reason and for what purpose are they in fact done? The idea behind them, if one looks a little more closely, is almost always practical! The exercisers are trying to find in them recovery from some infirmity which they have incurred through their hard and all too restless life. 'Exercises' are supposed to help to make people 'fit' again, healthy, successful and productive. They are supposed to enable them to meet the demands of the world equably, to parry the assaults of the world triumphantly, to endure stress without seizing up, to bear hurry and bustle without getting ill, to recover from overwork, etc. All this is very natural and understandable and can also be useful, provided that being practised in relaxation is not regarded – as an exerciser once put it – as 'important, after all, so that one can go on getting tensed up again for the rest of the day without becoming ill'. Then indeed relaxation exercises would fit without a break into the whole gamut of those means which sometimes seem to be the idea of modern industrial production: to manufacture on an ever greater scale means that enable human beings to stay painlessly in their wrong attitude! Then the whole thing becomes diabolical. Suffering becomes the justification of wrong ways.

Exercises have nothing to do with the *Way* insofar as they are done, as they are as a rule, in a *pragmatic* and not in an *initiatory* sense, i.e. in aid of the self-preservation of the external person and not of the development of the inner person. So, whenever there is talk of 'exercises', the first question to ask is '*How* are the exercises done, to what end are they done and *who* is doing them?' rather than '*What* is being practised?' This applies also in regard to a form of exercise that is becoming ever more widespread, the exercise of stillness.

People are coming together ever more frequently simply to be still with each other, to sit still and unmoving with each other – as for instance in the practice of Za-Zen, or even, without any special instruction in attitude, simply to sit still. Whether any object of contemplation is adopted in this exercise, a word, an image, a thought, or not, the main thing is being still.

There can be no doubt that this exercise represents something and is healing, healing in a profound sense of the word. It helps to make a person *whole* again. Even more far-reaching exercises in meditation should always begin with this exercise in *physical immobility*. Skill in this can become an art whose importance goes far beyond the blessing it represents for the physical body. As an exercise of the body that one is it contributes to the becoming-whole of the Person.

The enduring of physical immobility has very strict limits at first. Ten or even five minutes seem to beginners like an eternity. The more they then prolong the period of immobility, the closer comes the moment when they can do no more and feel like exploding. They get into a panic, into states that they can suppress only with an effort, or into a vacuum in which they are afraid of losing consciousness, and then in the nick of time comes a tickling in the throat or a desire to sneeze, a compulsion to cough or an unbearable pain, which provides the apparently legitimate excuse to interrupt or end, as though with a conditioned reflex, the 'stillness' that had finally become a 'cramp'. If, on the other hand, with the progress of training in immobility of this kind, disturbances are overcome and the exerciser can sit motionless (there is also the exercise of standing motionless in the hara) without difficulty, almost without limit and without going to sleep in the process – then it can be the prelude to effects that go deeper, *if* the exercise is carried out in the right spirit. But this is just where one must ask again: 'To what end is the exercise in stillness sought? There are three motives that are human and very natural, but which fall short nevertheless of the initiatory sense:

1 The exercisers are seeking in fact nothing but stillness, i.e. *repose from the 'bustle'* of the world, or, over and above that, to acquire a frame of mind in which, without losing inner stillness themselves, they can withstand the inner or outer bustle of their lives. This is an understandable concern. Its fulfilment, however – especially if it occurs without a settling of the unconscious – serves only to smooth and preserve the current façade of their world-I. But that is nothing for those who aspire beyond the limits of their I-horizon; indeed, like everything else that eases the possibility of living equably in the world, it can even delay or perhaps prevent their breaking out into the other Kingdom.

2 In the exercises in stillness, whatever their origin may be, people are seeking *beautiful experiences*. This again is a very understandable concern; and yet this very concern blocks the deeper blessing that a meditation exercise done in the right spirit can contain. The man and woman of our time, in their separation from the Essence, are in exile. So they are in search of their true, their infinite home, which only begins beyond the limits of their finite orders of existence and consciousness – and only when they have found it can it then be discovered also *within* those limits. The presence of our primordial home does indeed make itself known in our experience in certain blissful qualities of experience. So it is understandable that to them every means seems justified for overstepping the limits of their profane capacity for experience. And that is the idea of 'beautiful experiences', as they are being sought today in

drugs, in 'trips', in ecstatic dancing, as they always have been in alcohol and sexuality, and now also in exercises in stillness. The temptation to do this comes also, and not least, from the reading of texts in which, especially in the description of eastern meditation practices, ecstatic and wonderful states are reported, samadhi, satori and so on; laymen then think that such experiences, shattering all limits, blissful beyond measure, are the main promise contained in exercises in meditation. So they see the fulfilment of this promise as their real meaning. Yet this is very wide of the mark!

Just as great peace *can* be an outcome of long practice, so too in meditative 'practice' a blissful experience *can* sometimes occur – yet to make this the meaning of the exercise is to miss the meaning that is sought by those who are really aiming at the other Kingdom: the initiatory meaning, which aims at transformation.

3 A third concern drives the man and woman of our time to supposedly meditative exercises: the cultivation of '*higher faculties*'. 'But what has that to do with the *inner Way?*' That was the question with which an Eastern Master answered my own question about what he thought of the miraculous performances of the great fakirs. 'It would be a miracle', he said, 'if people who for decades, perhaps since childhood, indeed perhaps in their family for generations, had been practising the cultivation of "higher faculties" did not in the end achieve performances that to an unpractised person seemed like miracles. But what has that to do with the inner Way? Conversely, if someone advances along the inner Way to an ever higher stage, he too will be able to do things in the end which seem like miracles to others – but this happens incidentally, usually in secret. That is the very thing that shows the Master. He too may perhaps make use of miracles consciously on occasion, in order to awaken the other person, but he then forgoes them again, so that the other person should not get on to the wrong way, along which he might seek from the beginning what is due to him only at the end of the Way as the fruit of long maturing, and which may fall to him incidentally.'

So it is then: 'higher faculties' can arise through long practice in great stillness, but their development must not be the meaning of the exercise. For then in the last analysis the exercise would still be serving the power-hungry world-I, and . . . the Way would be missed. For, even if people intend to exercise their power to good ends, they are able to do so without harm 'to their soul' only when their pleasure- and power-seeking I has stepped back in token of the LIFE.

This observation does not rule out the possibility that the exercising of extrasensory faculties, such as telepathy or television for instance, i.e. the cultivation of a natural gift, which some people possess more than others – and which is being fostered today to a rapidly increasing extent by military and political secret services all over the world – can also be useful for the inner Way, and for the following reason: the testing of all extrasensory faculties presupposes a temporary elimination of the objectively fixing 'dualistic' consciousness. Because the capacity to overcome the predominance of the objective consciousness is a basic requirement for progress along the Way into the other dimension, any exercising of the non-objective consciousness can be beneficial. The meaning of such exercising then, however, is the realisation of a form of consciousness that is important for the initiatory person, because it aids transparence for transcendence, and not the faculty of clairvoyance or telaesthesia as such.

Meditation

Meditation as exercise along the spiritual Way fulfils its meaning only as exercise for transformation. The meaning of meditation as a transformation-exercise is a disposition in which people as whole persons, as mind, soul and body, become permeable for the divine Being dwelling in their Essence, able to become aware of it in their experience and to let it become manifest through them in the world. The meaning of meditation as transformation-exercise is the guaranteed permeability to the Being of people as Persons – so that the Being can sound forth (*personare*) in them and through them in the world. Person means a form permeable to the divine Being, a formed permeability of the whole man and woman to bear witness to their divine origin in their finite existence.

In the traditional sense we understand by meditation a spiritual exercise in which those doing it concentrate on a sacred word, an image, a passage from the Holy Scriptures, in brief on some objectivity given content, and contemplate it in a special manner and attitude. Meditation as objective contemplation, i.e. close occupation with a 'content' given over for deepened understanding and for deepened fulfilment, is and always will be one of the modes of spiritual exercise known as 'meditating'. But the decisive question is what effect such meditation has on the meditator.

If meditation, like all spiritual exercise, is to help people along the Way to their becoming-one with the Great Mystery, then it must be asked of this meditation, as of every other exercise, whether it merely enriches people through deepened understanding or whether it really *transforms* them.

And here we must ask ourselves: How can it happen that certain people, monks, for example, can meditate for years 'objectively' without really transforming themselves, i.e. without finding the breakthrough to the Essence, while those, on the other hand, whose meditating is done in the name of transformation can, in a meditation that goes beyond the phase of objective concentration, sometimes be subject to such a change in their whole disposition that when they open their eyes on coming out of the meditation a stone lying before them begins to shine from within! Why? Because in becoming free of all contents given to them objectively – i.e. from 'outside' – their inner eye, the Essence-eye, came open! What then has happened here? Simply that an object, a stone, by virtue of the transformation that took place in the person, has now been able to glow in the Essence concealed in its concrete nature! This can also happen to a picture, a sacred word. But that means, of course, that the opposition between objective and non-objective meditation, in the sense of an unbridgeable antagonism, rests on a misunderstanding; that the discrediting of non-objective meditation, which works via the void, as purely 'Eastern' is out of place; and that the demand that Christian meditation should stick unremittingly to the objective relation is misleading. Matters are the other way round: if it is the concern of Christian meditation, as of the Christian outlook in general, to perceive and unlock Creation, given to us and given over to us in the concrete nature of the world about us, as God's veiled presence, then that surely can only mean a way of perceiving in which the perceiver gets through the surface of the appearance to what is concealed and to what appears in concealment, to the eternally non-objective Essence, to the 'Word' of what is objectively given; frees it, as it were, for the experiencing person, from the prison of its objective veil, by making this permeable for its true core. But this the usual eye, which sees only objectively, cannot do.

So long as people fail even to emerge from the form of their natural, i.e. objective, consciousness – which they need to master their being-in-the-world but which, when it prevails exclusively, holds them back from perceiving the Supramundane in things – for so long will they be unable to approach things in a truly 'Christian' manner, i.e. one which perceives the *Word* in them. Then even 'meeting each other in Christ' remains an unfulfillable demand or an empty formula. They are able to reach the Essence in objects only to the degree that, in becoming empty of all contents, in becoming free of all somethings – images, thoughts, desires, ideas – they first become receptive within themselves for the touch of the 'Holy Ghost', the opener-of-eyes and preparer pure and simple. Because this is being understood today, the Zen exercises in stillness, Za-Zen, are becoming increasingly widespread. The void sought in them is no Eastern privilege. The difference is simply that for Buddhists the encounter and becoming-one with the ESSENCE (which they call the Buddha-nature) is the ultimate, whereas for Christians it is the experience of what they may and should then bear witness to also in the world, i.e. discover, release and make the principle of their living, loving and fashioning in the world. Becoming-one in the Essence is then a gateway, not the end.

Two sayings may accompany us along this Way, the saying of an Eastern Master and a saying of Novalis. The former, asked about the special character of Eastern wisdom, said: 'Wisdom looks inward, ordinary knowledge outward. But if one looks inward in the way that one looks outward, one turns the inside into an outside.' This saying cannot be taken seriously enough. 'Outward' – that means indeed 'objectively'. What is distilled in genuine wisdom, however, is something that only opens itself, and then 'intrinsically', if one is not looking for it a priori objectively. This insight must logically be carried further: one must learn to look outwardly in the way that one *should* look inwardly – intrinsically and non-objectively – so that one can come to see the Essence in the object. It is a matter, then, of an inside in the outside, of the inside present in every outside. And so from now on it is a matter of an outside that is to be perceived with regard to an inside.

The saying of Novalis runs: 'Everything visible is something invisible raised into a state of mystery.' This saying can be varied: 'Everything audible is something inaudible raised into a state of mystery. Everything given in space and time, something beyond space and time raised into a state of mystery. Everything mundane, finite, something Supramundane, infinite, raised into a state of mystery' – and it is precisely in this raised-into-a-state-of-mystery that human beings share by virtue of their infinite origin! And so true and wonderful as the saying is about prayer: '*Prayer is the expression of the infinite longing of the finite creature for its infinite origin*', so true and not to be refused is the demand that those who have been called to the Way have the mission to seek, find and bear witness to the Infinite in the finite. The transformation to the disposition in which people are able to do this is the meaning of the Great Meditation and, inseparable from it, of the meditative life!

The meditative life

To bear witness to the Infinite in the finite – that presupposes an insight that is to be gained indeed only in a meditative basic attitude: that the whole 'world' which we experience, and in the centre of it we ourselves, can be perceived as an infinite attempt of the Infinite to appear in the finite! Every object, every flower, every tree, every animal, every human being, as that which is and lives, is bursting with the power of the LIFE, which seeks to become manifest without end, to come forth in it and appear in a particular shape. Some time or other those who have awakened to the Essence can experience as certainty, in a significant moment that fills them with consternation and at the same time with bliss, that they too share in this LIFE, which as the Divine would like to regenerate itself even in them and through them in a unique human way. What else should the saying mean, that we *are* the sons of God, but possible *experience*, *promise* and *mission*? As sons of God we are *ourselves* the quite-Other in respect of the 'world' and at the same time the LIFE taking shape in it. We are so, then, not in opposition to it, but called to prove ourselves, in ourselves, against it and in it, *as* the 'quite-Other', kept veiled at first, but destined to become manifest. In those who have awakened to the Way this is no pious saying, but knowledge warm as blood, pulsing through their days and nights – as experience, promise and mission.

The infinite inborn in us in its drive to appear in the finite, that is our true centre! To *open* towards it, to *keep* in contact with it, to *live* to it and from it, *in* the midst of the world, in the midst of what conceals the centre from us, that purely and simply is the meaning of the meditative state. And it is not confined to separate exercise, let alone to sitting still in meditation. The meditative state is not to be distinguished from non-meditative being-in-the-world as a doing-nothing from doing. It appears rather as a doing-nothing in doing, a still, keeping-in-contact-with and responsible-to the Being, even in the midst of the bustle of achievement. Only thus can even sword-fighting, archery, sculpting or tree-felling be a meditative doing; and 'every situation', as an ancient Buddhist saying has it, 'becomes the best of all opportunities' to show fidelity to the Being in the midst of existence, hence by 'living every moment like a piece of eternity'.

The five stages

When pupils on the initiatory Way are able to perceive themselves rightly in the body, and have understood and can permit the right centre of gravity, the right relation between tension and relaxation and right breathing, they are ready to start the transformation via the body which is what the Way is about: the transformation to a *permeable form* for the Essence. This is also the true meaning of all spiritual exercise, and especially of exercise in meditation.

Experience teaches that the form of being-a-Person which is sought along the initiatory Way is the result of a movement of transformation which, viewed schematically, takes place in five steps.

1   The first step is concerned with getting free of the dominance of the

world-I, which holds on to its positions. This requires in the first place a letting-go of everything which the I, turned to the world, is at one with, everything to which it holds fast. People must let go of themselves with their theoretical and ethical ideas and systems. They must give up their self-will and also that heart of theirs whose love consists in clinging. This *letting-go* (in the body this means letting-go 'above', i.e. in the shoulders) is followed by a *letting-down* elsewhere (in the body, into the pelvic basin). This letting-down ends in a complete letting-oneself-into and trustful *letting-oneself-become-one* with the 'Ground'! The Ground which people have to let themselves into receives them only to the degree that they are in the *hara*. Hara means then the pelvic basin, the vessel that receives and transforms what is to be let go and those who are letting go of themselves.

The movement of transformation that takes place in the hara has in itself three steps: first the receiving of those who are letting go of themselves into the *maternal vessel*; second, the downward opening of the pelvic basin, which permits the inflowing of the cosmic forces, through which a cleansing takes place from all objective contents in a union with Great Nature. This is the function of the hara as *cosmic vessel*. Third, in becoming empty of all objects, the *virgin vessel* is created, turned upwards again; its inner presence opens people to receive the 'spiritual Spirit'. These three steps in the development of the hara from the maternal, via the cosmic to the virgin vessel together constitute the first step in the initiatory movement of transformation, as it is practised in the meditation exercise of sitting in order to become empty.

2   The second step is to experience the inflowing of the spiritual Spirit: to experience a Light that orders everything anew, charged with the incipient forms of a new life; to become one with a Spirit that, beyond all customary orders, images, thoughts and conceptions, fructifies those who are now ready to receive.

3   The fruit of this union of 'heaven and earth' – and this fulfils the third step – is to experience *rebirth as a child of heaven and earth*. The 'place' of this experience is the *heart*. This is not the heart that sits on the left, which clings, but the heart in the centre, which represents those who have become free, who have come to themselves. With this experience, when it occurs, the highest point seems to have been reached of what is possible. People feel born anew. How understandable it is that at this point they are filled with the desire to keep to themselves, shielded from any disturbance by the world, which is inimical to the Supramundane. Yet at this very point there is another demand; for this transformation experience is not enough to produce transformed people, an enlightenment is not enough to give birth to people who are enlightened.

4   Weak and without shells, as new-born creatures are, they cannot yet fulfil their mission in the world – angels have never yet changed the

world. In order to become capable of proving themselves as 'sons of God' in the world, such people must now – and this is the fourth step – work on the transformation according to plan. To that end they must go back 'into the world'; they must risk the destruction of what they have just gained; they must, to put it metaphorically, take up the fight against the dragon, and harden themselves, bathing in the dragon's blood, for the fight against all the forms the Adversary takes in the world. The 'dark' against which the newly born, i.e. those awakened to the Essence, must take their stand is also their own shadow. Nowhere do people encounter the dark places of their own soul so unavoidably and with such terrible clarity as in the mirror of the divine Light that has dawned in them.

5 The fruit of this integration of the 'dark world', of the fourth step, of the 'Quaternity' (C. G. Jung), appears, and this is the fifth step, as the quintessence: the *tempered heart*, tempered in the encounter with the dark 'outside' and 'inside', by virtue of which alone people are capable, as examples of a higher order of *homo faber*, of fulfilling their mission of bearing witness to the Being in existence. The initiatory Way ends for the Christian West not in the redeeming All-ONE, but through this in the Complete Person, freed by it from the I-spell and made capable of bearing individual witness to his or her heavenly origin.*

* Cf. J. W. Klein, *Ihr seid Götter*, Neske-Verlag, 1967.

VIII

Proving grounds

Everyday life as practice

The main proving ground opens up along the Way as soon as people are ready, and truly resolved, to conduct their lives in the world in the light of their destiny, i.e. in service to the supramundane Being. They have from then on to bear witness to their infinite origin in the finite existence. They must have understood that only in fidelity to this service can they become whole. So long as they live only for their security, their happiness and their service to the world, they will not be able to find what is right. Only when what matters to them is the coming to manifestation of the LIFE in the world in *all* knowing, working and serving, will they arrive on the Way. And then everyday life will be tranformed into a single ground for practice. So long as people seek something for themselves in practice, whatever it may be, the gaining of higher faculties, beautiful experiences or just tranquillity, harmony or even their own well-being, but also when they are occupied in doing some work without reference to the Being, they will miss the Way.

Everyday life as practice means continual turning inwards and turning about, letting go of the world, and letting in the Essence. And once we feel the innermost core of our own Self, once the Essence awakens in us, we sense also the Essence in objects, and in the midst of worldly existence we are met by the Being on all sides.

When the Essence enters our inner being we feel different. We are relaxed and released, charged with power, clear and filled with generative Life. What was a burden to us just before loses its weight; what had just filled us with fear afflicts us no more. What was plunging us into despair loses its sting. Where everything was obstructed, everything now seems open. Where we had just been poor, we feel rich, and in the midst of all bustle it becomes within us strangely peaceful and still. We feel as though bathed in an invisible Light, which makes us clear and warm, and we find ourselves in a glow that shines through everything. All this can suddenly be there, and yet vanish again just as quickly. We cannot bring it about or retain it, but if we have paid heed to it rightly we can become aware of the attitudes that prevent such experiences and equally of the other one that prepares us for such an event, and practise the latter, not only at special times but the whole day.

The world in which we live is not a vale of tears that keeps us away from the mountain-tops of the Divine, but a bridge that links us to it. We only have to clear through the mist of consciousness that denies us sight of it and tear down the walls that bar our way to it. That is the meaning of the demand that we live everyday life as practice. For that no special time is needed. Every moment calls us to reflection and to trial. And there is no activity, whatever outward purpose it may serve, that may not hold the chance for us to give ourselves ever more deeply to the truth. Whatever we are doing, whether we are walking, standing or sitting, whether we are writing, talking or remaining silent, whether we are on the attack or defending ourselves, helping or serving, whatever work it may be – everything and anything harbours within it the chance of doing it in an attitude and approach that bear witness to, establish and strengthen contact with the Being more and more, and thus serve to increase *transparence* for *transcendence.*

When everyday life is lived as practice the 'wheel of change' turns at every moment, as in all spiritual exercise that does not fail in its aim, in five steps according to the same law: 1 the proving of one's critical vigilance; 2 giving away and giving up whatever stands in the way of one's becoming permeable; 3 becoming one with the transforming Ground; 4 becoming new through the internal image that arises from it; 5 bearing witness and putting to the proof in everyday life (any lack of success being noted again by one's critical vigilance).

Every separate part of this rotation serves in its own way the forming of the disposition in which human beings become progressively transparent for the Being. None of the steps must be lacking. Each, if it is really carried out, contains all the other steps. And yet each step has its own meaning. So it is as well for a beginner – and who does not remain one all his or her life? – whether in everyday life or in special practice periods, to place the emphasis now on this step, now on that. One thing, however, must never be forgotten: that there is change only when the wheel of change remains in motion. Every step becomes fruitful only within the continual turning of the wheel. Maturing means eternal revolution.

The strength for the turning that is never to be broken never comes from the one 'experience' in which the Being, at some special moment, stirred us, redeeming and binding us. The meaning of the impulse that was experienced 'to bear witness to the Being in existence' must, rather, be constantly recognised and grasped anew by us, its fulfilment constantly affirmed in new resolution, established in the conscience and incorporated into the will. And only through fidelity to 'change without end' is there any existentially valid vigilance, letting go, giving away, becoming one, becoming new and bearing witness in everyday life.

Fellow-feeling

The ignorant often ask whether the 'inner Way' along which human beings 'turned inward', trouble themselves over their Essence, and seek again and again to find contact with it and keep it under all circumstances, does not turn them in on themselves in such a way that they no longer have any sense of what is happening around them and lose sight more or less egocentrically of their fellow human beings and their community. This question alone shows lack of experience in the one who asks it.

The 'Essence' that comes into the centre of responsible consciousness on the initiatory Way simply isn't the 'ego' that sets itself off from everything with its 'I am I and will remain so, distinguishing myself from others and deciding against them'; it is, on the contrary, the way in which we share in the One that is present in every living thing. So to the very degree that the 'Essence' unfolds in, and as, our inner being, with awareness of being at one in the Essence in our relations with our fellow humans and the world, consciousness dawns in us of being linked to one another, dependent on one another and given over to one another – but naturally at a new, i.e. initiatory, level! It is true that when people arrive on the initiatory Way, really enter upon it, this does mean a total revolution, a turning 'inwards', which may even cause them for a while to seek solitude. But it is an age-old misunderstanding that the great revolution can be represented as the perfecting of a personality that stands egocentrically in the world and without love. Even an ideological materialist, on the other hand, can be absorbed in selfless service to society, with the aim of the greatest security and the greatest affluence for the greatest number, and so can do much good humanly speaking; and yet this has nothing whatever to do with the inner Way in the initiatory sense. That the latter can manifest itself *also* in a form of life that appears 'ethical' is not to say that this is characteristic of its nature. Rightly understood, Christianity is more than consummate social work, and the meaning of Christ's cross is something different from a 'Red Cross' exalted into the meaning of life.

When people arrive on the inner Way, i.e. when they grasp all at once, on the basis of an experience of the Essence, what they are actually charged with most inwardly, their whole life is changed. As 'pupils on the Way' they have become different people; they see life with different eyes and hence differently from before – and this affects those around them no less than themselves. Everything now receives its meaning and its significance only from their relation to the *Being*. So previous connections, friendship, long-standing ties become for the most part questionable; family, blood relations, worldly associations lose some of their unquestioned binding force. Since those who are touched and called by the Essence revolve thenceforth about a new centre, they withdraw from everything which, by that yardstick, is peripheral. They then often seem to others strangely altered, disloyal and perhaps no longer quite normal. For those who have once experienced the twofold origin of their humanity, who have felt their heavenly origin as promise and accepted it as mission, their relations with their fellow human beings and the world are radically changed. They no longer share the joys and sorrows of this *world* with other people as much as before, but they associate with them as brothers and sisters on the *Way* into the Kingdom that is not of the world! This means that they stand with others and for others in the other dimension, i.e. in the experience, in the promise and in the mission of bearing witness to it in this world, also and precisely in the togetherness of life. 'Fellow-feeling' acquires a new meaning, in which the 'heavenly' origin of humankind ceases to be merely a matter of pious belief.

Those whose life is ruled by the Way inevitably attract others who are looking for the Way; for their manner of reacting to whatever it may be, entering into conversation about this, and not about that, and also their manner of inquiry, directs the attention of others involuntarily to what matters 'at bottom' also to them, but of which they only now become conscious. In no time the one finds himself, or herself, in the following of the other, and seekers of the Way soon becomes companions along the Way.

One's fellow human beings! For the 'Modern Age' that is coming to an end these words have no great repute. They contradicted and contradict a world ruled by Reason. The spirit of such a world is hard and soulless, material and with no room for feelings. For the cold spirit of our time 'fellow-feeling' has something too warm about it, too soft, which smacks of compassion. It means something like *caritas*. This word creates uneasiness, for some people because it reminds them of what they ought to practise but don't; for others because they want no compassion, but only what is their due. Fellow-feeling in the new sense is an obeisance to the other in his Essence.

   Human beings are dialogically constructed. Human life takes place as call and answer. But the question is: At what level? Who calls and who answers? When people discover themselves anew in the Essence, i.e. at a new level, they also discover their fellow humans anew, as partners and as mission, as companions of the Way and as brothers and sisters along the Way. For those who as yet know nothing of the Way, call and answer take place only at the level of the 'world' and its concerns and needs. But the fact that set eternally alongside and above this call–answer relationship is the calling forth and calling home by God, 'Adam, where art thou?', and that only as answer to this call do human beings become wholly human and wholly fellow humans – that is something which is recognised only by those for whom the 'inner ear' has opened. Only when, in the relationship between human being and fellow human, the supramundane Life becomes the significant and guiding factor can the relationship of human to human become right and fruitful in the deepest sense. For a life of fellow-feeling can be completely fulfilled only when its true meaning is discovered: to disclose – in the midst of the world – the Supramundane in the other, i.e. to exercise love; not, however, a love that is 'lovey-dovey', but one which, in service to the Being, releases, encourages and makes fruitful. The supramundane Life and its witnesses are anything but 'lovey-dovey'.

To show fellow-feeling means at the level of the natural man and woman helping others to satisfy the three basic impulses of life, towards security, meaning and shelter, in a form that corresponds to their natural world-I. This means helping others towards a secure life, helping them to find a meaningful place in service to their work or community, comforting them in distress and helping them to find shelter in the love of a worldly community. Every role or situation in which one person meets another offers an opportunity to satisfy this fellow-human duty to the worldly existence of the other. One has only to have it in mind.

But just as people are not identical with their world-I, but only become completely themselves when they gain conscious contact with their supramundane Essence, so too is genuine fellow-feeling fulfilled only when it is proved in the light of the supramundane Essence. We must distinguish clearly between the fellow-human duty that falls to us in respect of the worldly chances and existential need of another as a world-I conditioned by destiny, and the other duty that arises for us with regard to the other person's Essence, overshadowed or repressed by this I, and the distress and promise that it causes him or her. So one can acquire obligations to another in two different ways: as a companion in destiny and as a brother or sister.

Fellow-feeling in the higher sense then means, however, recognising and becoming aware of one another in the truth of our heavenly origin, with the love that, in the name of the sacred spirit, i.e. experienced as Supramundane, and its Light dwelling within us, can also be strict and severe in the breaking down of nice façades which, under the pretext of securing a smoother and harmonious life in the world, prevent the Supramundane from becoming manifest.

Growing old

For those who are bound up in the enticements, sorrows and obligations of this world the Supramundane as a rule is only something that comes in at quiet moments, or appears or is summoned in extreme situations. When people grow old in the right way the meshes of the net that holds us fast in purely worldly relations become wider, and what previously appeared only rarely and as something extra, now presses in ever more frequently as what is real – provided that ageing people can let go, and that they let in what awaits them.

So the twofold origin of human beings makes itself felt in a special way when their growing old means not ageing but maturing. In becoming one with their heavenly origin, what is conditioned by space and time loses in significance and what is beyond space and time comes to the fore. For people who are on the Way the Supramundane shines ever more clearly through the walls of worldly existence, which become ever thinner. In the way in which they look upon life, accept with tranquillity whatever it brings or takes away, and seize the chance in every situation of bearing witness to a higher meaning, it becomes evident that with them a quite different, higher LIFE is gaining ground.

Whenever life is still whole, or has become so again, it is permeable for a higher Life. This transparence for the divine Being pressing to become manifest in us and through us, which is ultimately the goal of all spiritual development, becomes for old people, if they continue to mature, the true meaning and finally the only meaning of their existence.

The meaning of old age, like its dignity, is no longer attached to an outward activity, producing an effect in the world, but to transparence for the divine Being dwelling within us, which as an inner Light shines out as supramundane power, wisdom and goodness. The fruit of mature humanity is the blessing of a radiation that issues from a person without any activity, beyond either activity or inactivity.

Human life can be rounded off in the deepest sense only by those who to the end keep on increasing and maturing. Conversely, whenever we stand still and cling to what has already come to be, especially to certain ideas which we have once formed for ourselves about our life and its meaning, we close ourselves to what is seeking to come out, in us and through us, to the light from our deepest Essence. Hardened against the longing of our own hearts we fall inevitably into terrible fear and end our lives bitter and without hope. But when ageing people accept their growing old and are ready to change to the end, they can find that the very decline of their natural powers makes it easier for something supernatural to emerge in them. They can feel – when they let go and submit to it – how another, greater Life is speaking to them from within and, if they learn to listen, is giving them the bliss of a completely new quality of life. When the heart detaches itself from everything to which it clings, a fullness and power begin to make themselves felt which are not of this world. It is a mystery which, quite independently of poverty, ill health and loneliness, bestows riches, support and shelter. Full of amazement, those around such people can then see how in a strange way they change and clear. Instead of becoming hard, bitter and taciturn, a burden to themselves and others, they become ever more relaxed; they become serene, cheerful and kindly. What is it that is being expressed here? That such people are outgrowing their worldly nature, rooted in their earthly origin – which is bound to suffer from the ending of its little life – and through awareness of their supramundane Essence-nature, which testifies to their heavenly origin and is now emerging to the light, they are becoming new people, happily for them and for others. In such testimony to the divine Being dwelling within us, old age rounds itself off in mature humanity and bears a fruit that bestows blessings, a fruit which now unintentionally and quite without effort falls like a ripe apple from the tree. This fruit is the hidden work of the inner Way.

All the reality of this world, insofar as human beings comprehend and also master it, is only the 'profane', the approaches to the temple of a deeper Reality. This Reality is no longer subject to us, as the world is in the freedom of the mind, which overcomes our bondage in respect of our primordial nature; on the contrary, it is *we* who are subject to the Reality that now dawns in us. Yet if we prove ourselves as *its* servants, it makes us masters of this world in an entirely new sense, by enabling us to perceive the world in such a way that in the midst of its relations, remote from God, it comes to know itself in its supramundane Essence and begins to create the conditions in which the Supramundane can take shape.

Ageing people live towards death. The way in which they take it reveals their maturity.

The nearness of death reveals the nearing *of the Life* from which we come and into which we go back again, and which, even for the period of this life, has never let us go. But what has usually moved us during our life only in the unconscious seeks in old age to come more and more into consciousness. And people age in the right way who permit this coming-into-consciousness. Then in the end the meaning of their earthly form shines out more and more, to be the *medium* which, even in contradiction to the Being, lets it speak.

Dying and death

How people dies depends upon how they have lived. So different are the lives of human beings, so different are their deaths. People's attitude to death reflects their attitude to life. As their lives come to an end it becomes evident what people have understood by 'life' and whether in the last analysis they have lived more from their heavenly or from their earthly origin.

For those who believe that life in space and time is all there is, suffering has no sense and death is only an enemy. They are afraid of death. For those who have learnt to sense already through this space-time life the other, supramundane Life, life in time has already become a proving of the LIFE which is at work in and above all time and which is beyond life and death. It becomes a living towards the LIFE that leaves death behind it. Yet this LIFE only dawns in people to the degree that their life, which is in time, can cease. This is already so during life-time and it is the true meaning of all dying, even physical death. In living and dying the LIFE grows in people's consciousness to the degree that their consciousness oversteps the horizon of their world-I.

By virtue of their heavenly origin, human beings belong to the LIFE that is beyond life, which is inherent with death. Only in suffering from the limitation of this life does consciousness of the Great LIFE awaken in human beings, does it become conscious of itself in humans. Only in suffering to the point of breakdown do human beings gain the strength to testify to IT in space and time. The greatest testimony to the LIFE is given by those who are lit by IT in dying.

In dying, the elementary I asserts itself once more quite strongly. Arrived at the limit of its life, it once more gathers up all the forces of nature in order to hold on to this life. It also happens often enough that in themselves people have been fully prepared for death, and yet have still not been spared the throes of death. Yet precisely when this rebellion against death is strong the Greater Life can dawn in a special way as the I comes to an end. Only at the limit are we very near to what lies beyond the limit, so in the darkness of the end the gleam of a beginning can meet us, and at the agonising end of the finite the Infinite can find us, relieving us of all agony.

When ministers concern themselves sympathetically with those who are dying, they see those who are doomed to death as fellow human beings, who like themselves suffer in their world-I and are afraid of death. When they place themselves in a fellow-human way by their side in their distress at death, they help the dying, without reserve and in full confidence, to unburden themselves of all that is weighing upon them. They can absolve themselves and confess what is troubling them, and ask for what they want. When those in attendance open themselves quite simply in a fellow-human way – perhaps by speaking to the dying also of their own distress and their own guilt – they help the dying to rid themselves of all the shackles that have held them prisoner to the last as an 'imposing' world-I. They help them to free themselves from the delusion that they can even cross the threshold in an 'impressive' manner. And so they help them to arrive at the inner truth, to let fall all façades and now open themselves naked and simple to what is coming to them unavoidably as the great Unknown.

But those who attend the dying can go a step further: they can associate with them from Essence to Essence, as brother or sister in the Being. In that case they must not get held up in feelings of fellow-human sympathy at the distress of death. But neither should they give purely impersonal testimony, beyond all personal distress, to the promise of faith. They should rather, in devoutly loving, but also strict regard for the other's Essence, summon them into being their true self, should set them, possibly by silence, within the bounds of the truth and fortify them to bear the painful extinction of their I, now finally suffering at having to let go, in view of something quite different. This can then be a help for the shining out, at the end of existence in this worldly life, of the glory of the supramundane Life.

To be present in accordance with the Essence at the extinguishing of an I makes the highest demands on the attending person. As at the beginning so too at the end of life human beings need a midwife. Such helpers cannot relieve others either of the birth itself or of its pains. They can only help to create the conditions in which the fruit of the body, which in dying has become open to conceive and is now perhaps pregnant, can come to light. For this they must stand the test of a higher, a supra-personal love. For the sake of it they must themselves forgo, which is often hard enough, the minor demonstration of love, which expresses sympathy only in a worldly sense. There is the love that in the world heals wounds, relieves cares, dries tears and even lies out of love, simply to relieve or lighten human suffering. This love no longer has any place here. One should not spare the dying the pain of the truth. The truth itself is always less terrible than the fear of it. And is it not precisely someone who is dying, more than anyone else, who is entitled to the truth?

Dying can be the chance for a last or perhaps the first proving of full humanity and the greatest test of personal freedom. The dying can either try to preserve themselves once more in defiant self-assertion or, out of freedom, full of trust and without reserve, abandon themselves to a higher power. They have the freedom to persist obdurately in their old view, in their natural right to life and in their lack of faith, or, on the other hand, in the presentiment of a higher meaning and a grace touching them at this very time, open themselves unconditionally and without reserve to something that to them is as yet Unknown. They can, in a No to what is happening to them, finally and completely harden themselves and shut themselves up within themselves or, on the other hand, with the last spark of their freedom, consciously submit themselves to the stream of infinite love that is already pressing powerfully within them.

Over all the abysmal happenings of death shines inexorably, demand-ingly and full of promise the cool star of truth. It is the truth of the infinite origin, demanding the end of the finite. Because it is this truth, people are able not only to experience it at this moment as a harsh summons, but also sense it as the promise of a deliverance that is bearing them towards a new existence. It is true, the nearness of death brings the I, clinging to life, on to the scene once more. But that is the very moment when those in attendance must let the voice of truth begin to sound, insistently and without fear of pain for the other. For, however the dying may view what is coming to them, it is the moment of truth. Only thus may they perhaps gain the freedom to say Yes, in order then to discover perhaps that approaching death, which breaks all barriers, opens the door to all-dissolving Love, which can now stream in quite unexpectedly. Even a hint of the truth can, by way of a moment of terror, bring the Essence into the inner being, and death has lost its terror.

I shall never forget one such experience. A friend was close to death after a serious operation. The doctors, who knew this very well, had assured him that he could expect to leave hospital the following week in order to prepare himself for another operation, which would make him quite well again. This was what I too was told by his relations, who were keeping watch by his bedside. I went in and saw the lie. The man was already marked by death. I sent his wife out, so as to be alone with him. He spoke of his hopes of being able to give a lecture shortly, as planned, or at least of being able to dictate it in time, so that someone else could read it for him. It could be clearly felt how behind these words was a falsity that was sensed even by him. So I plucked up courage and said: 'My dear friend, I think you would do better, instead of thinking about your lecture, to let everything go for once and set your mind on the point that lies beyond life and death. Do you hear me,' I repeated, 'beyond life and *death*.' The effect of these words was moving. He closed his eyes. A new life came into his face. His ashen colour gave way to a rosy glow. A luminosity flowed over his countenance. Then he opened his eyes, and with an expression of infinite peace stretched out his hand to me and just said, quite simply: 'Thank you.' Then he closed his eyes again; I left and told his wife that she could reckon on only a few more days. However, the dying of this man, who was not afraid of death and had the maturity to prepare himself for it with a clear mind, was spoilt. The nearer the moment came for passing over, the time, therefore, when he needed the greatest peace, peaceful communion with his life's companion and peace, peace, peace for himself, so much the more assiduous was the coming and going of the nurses and the setting in motion of the medical apparatus, including technical apparatus, in order to prolong purely physical life for a few more hours. So in his last hour this man had taken from him the last thing that he might still have been able to call his own: his death.

Why don't we let people die in peace when the moment has come?

Why make it so hard for people in dying to enter their heavenly home and the radiance of a new life?

Epilogue

We are of twofold origin, infinite and finite, heavenly and earthly. Yet where are we really at home?

There is the experience of coming home from exile in the mundanely conditioned into the supramundane Unconditioned. This occurs quite without cause as a sudden awakening and as the experience of being saved from the distress of death, and of the despair and desolation of this life, in the sudden knowledge of a LIFE immanent within us which is beyond life and death, beyond dark and light, beyond loneliness and community. There is the experience of the heavenly origin as our true home which we become aware of when we are able to free ourselves from the dominance of our world-I and let that from which it separates us come into us. It separates us from the Essence, in which we share in the LIFE, which in us and through us would like to become manifest in the world, manifest as creative-redemptive power, as conscience and as a love that is not of this world.

We are in our Essence children of the divine Being, citizens of the Kingdom that is not of this world, brothers and sisters of the Lord. We can become conscious of this, startled and happy and released for new responsibility, if only we can extricate ourselves from the dominance of that within us which separates itself and sets itself off from our primordial home in the Essence. It is the I which separates itself and says: 'I am I and will remain so.' It is the I which from its I-standing turns everything it sees into an ob-ject, something standing opposite. It is the I which fixes, revolves about what is established and establishes even what cannot by its nature be established. It is the I which, with its will to endure, resists each change along the Way, which resists the fundamental law of all life, the eternal 'dying and becoming', the eternal going forth and going in, and as such *is* the sin against the LIFE. It is in the consciousness centred in this I that the infinite congeals into the finite, that the supramundane Being beyond space and time veils itself in space-time existence! So it is not because it is mortal that our life is finite, for in the 'dying and becoming' of the leaves lies indeed the life of the eternal tree. And what to us appears contrary and finite *is* the Infinite, One in the prism of the divisive I. So the finite origin is nothing else but the product of this I, the way in which the Infinite conceals itself in the eye of the world-I.

'Finite origin' does not mean that we are begotten of fleshly parents. If it did the whole abundance of the earthly world would be of 'earthly origin'. No, the earth itself is of heavenly origin. Precisely *in* its becoming–dying–becoming is it evidence of the eternal LIFE. The finite origin of humankind is the generative act in which the Infinite congeals in the consciousness of mankind into the finite without end, in which the Unconditioned conceals itself in the conditioned in space and time, and the Essence in the world-I. Finite existence is a contradiction not only of the infinite Being, but also of mankind, the place of the Being's self-manifestation, where it veils itself in a human way and via suffering from its concealment reveals itself in a human way.

Yet – blessed art thou, my sinful I; for without you, without the suffering from separation, how would I know of the One which you obstruct, of my infinite origin, and where, if not in your renegade world, would I be able to prove my fidelity to my home, the Infinite, and testify to the only One that is?

Only in suffering from the finite in the case of the Infinite, only in straining for the Infinite in the case of the finite, does each become aware of itself, and so the Whole living in both becomes experience, promise and mission for manifestation in human shape.